Mrs Merton's

World of Television

Mrs Merton's World of Television

CAROLINE AHERNE, CRAIG CASH,

HENRY NORMAL & DAVE GORMAN

Hodder & Stoughton

Copyright © 1997 Caroline Aherne, Craig Cash, Henry Normal and Dave Gorman

First published in Great Britain in 1997 by Hodder & Stoughton
A division of Hodder Headline PLC

The right of Caroline Aherne, Craig Cash, Henry Normal and Dave Gorman to be
identified as the Authors of the Work has been asserted by them in accordance
with the Copyright, Designs and Patents Act 1988.

10 9 8 7 6 5 4 3 2 1

British Library Cataloguing in Publication Data
A CIP catalogue record for this title is available from the British Library

ISBN 0 340 69654 0

Design and artwork by The Bridgewater Book Company
Art Director: Stephen Parker
Mac Artwork: Richard Constable, Ginny Zeal
Photography: Matt Squires and Ian Parsons
Illustration: Paul Allen, Paul Collicut, Ivan Hissey,
Simeon Stout and Curtis Tappenden

Printed and bound in Great Britain by
Butler and Tanner Ltd, Frome and London

Hodder & Stoughton
A division of Hodder Headline PLC
338 Euston Road
London NW1 3BH

Dedicated to all friends of Dorothy

Contents

Mrs Merton's WHO'S WHO of TV

All you need to know about the world's top twenty-six TV celebrities, conveniently arranged in alphabetical order

ADIE, KATE The Forces sweetheart. Adds a bit of glamour to war-torn areas.

BUSHELL, GARY Incisive wit and literary genius or brain-dead bearded buffoon? Nobody dares to say!

CHAS See below

DAVE See above

EVANS, CHRIS Children's entertainer. The new Timmy Mallett.

FERGIE Highly-acclaimed children's author who unfairly suffers from bad publicity involving a previous relationship which the Press refuse to forget.

GREER, GERMAINE The less said about her the better.

HASSELHOFF, DAVID Famous for single-handedly championing the feminist cause by showing that scantily-clad beauties can save lives just as well as paunchy middle-aged men.

INMAN, JOHN Versatile character actor. Best known for his camp shop assistant roles. In recent years his catchphrase 'I'm free!' has never been more apt.

JANUS, SAMANTHA Bright actress who realized that adding the letter J to the start of her surname would greatly enhance her career prospects.

KILROY-SILK, ROBERT Leathery-looking presenter of topical discussion programme. Famed for his sympathetic wringing of tears from any audience member, no matter how callous this may look to the viewing public.

LULU The third Krankie.

MONTALBAN, RICARDO Apparently famous for a small tattoo on his bottom.

NAIL, JIMMY In my opinion he is as hard as his name suggests. Immortalized in the Shirley Bassey song, 'Big Spender'.

ORANGE, JASON Since the demise of the popular youth combo Take That, Jason has successfully set up his own mobile phone network.

PAXMAN, JEREMY Game show host of the highest order. His catchphrase, 'No conferring' has gripped the nation's playgrounds.

QUINTEN, CHRIS Left a dead-end job playing loveable mechanic Brian Tilsley in the nation's favourite soap when he spotted an opening in the lucrative mobile DJ market.

RANTZEN, ESTHER Television has never filled the vacuum left by That's Life, with its ever popular mix of genitalia-shaped vegetables, singing dogs and unfortunate typographical errors. It never waned in what seemed like a sixty-year run.

SELLECK, TOM At one time so popular his moustache was adopted by both the gay and lesbian communities.

TRAVIS, DAVE LEE Wisely never peaked on TV by restricting his appearances to other people's shows. Unfortunately he was never as astute in his radio career.

USTINOV, PETER Made a living out of people not quite knowing what he does but presuming whatever it is to be clever.

VORDERMAN, CAROL Famous for adding, subtracting and dividing, and being fully conversant with every letter of the alphabet whether it be vowel or consonant.

WATERMAN, PETER A poor man's Peter Stringfellow.

ZIPPY One arm, no legs and a zip across his mouth, and still more interesting than Channel 5.

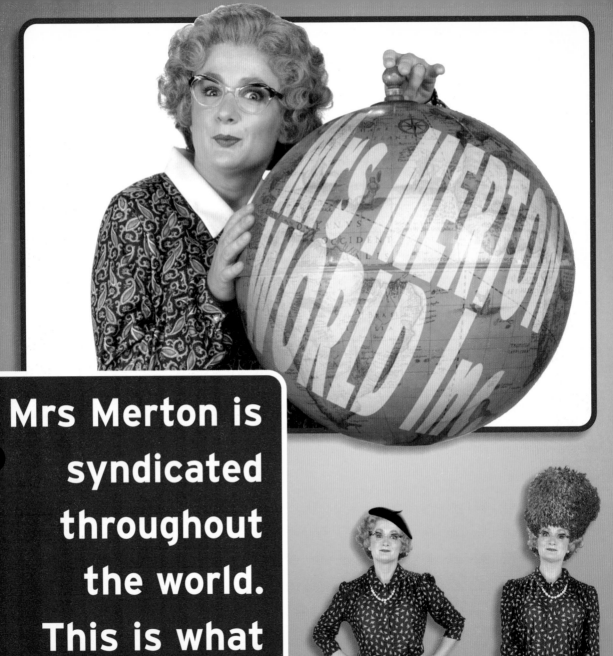

Mrs Merton is syndicated throughout the world. This is what she looks like on foreign TV →

FRANCE
Madame Merton

RUSSIA
Mrs Mertonov

WALES
Merton the Chat

AUSTRALIA
Sheila Merton

GERMANY
Frau Merton

MEXICO
El Merto

HOLLAND
Mrs Van Merton

COCKNEY
Mrs gone for a
burton

CHINA
風水

SCOTLAND
Mrs McMerton

how *TV* was INVENTED

At the turn of the last century, a young boffin named JOHN LOGIE BAIRD sat by the wire- less wishing that as well as listening to Gloria Hunniford, he

SPECIAL LAR

could see her too. He decided there and then to invent television. It was almost midnight by the time young John Logie had finished, by which time all the good programmes had been on. Fortunately he didn't miss them, as three days earlier he had invented the video.

E PRINT PAGE

A Typical Day in the Life of *Cilla*

Cilla Black, Liverpool

8.08 a.m. Cilla wakes up in a four-poster bed with Bobby by her side whistling the theme tune to Blind Date.

8.09 a.m. The phone rings. It's our Graham with a quick reminder to say what a national treasure Cilla is.

8.59 a.m. The door bell rings. It's the *Sun*. They want to do a front page scoop of twenty things you never knew about that hat.

9.30 a.m. Cilla rings an 0151 number and asks them to remind her of the accent for next week's show.

10.15 a.m. Breakfast. Champagne, pop tarts and caviar.

10.29 a.m. Cilla reprimands Bobby for over-consoling the two young girl contestants who weren't chosen last week.

11.03 a.m. Flowers arrive from Jimmy Tarbuck with the usual message: 'We've both done so well for a pair of talentless Scousers. PS. I'm off to the golf course with Lynchey.'

11.35 a.m. Nicky Clarke arrives for Cilla's daily rinse. Bobby's beard gets a trim due to a special 'Two For One' offer.

1.00 p.m. Cilla and Stan Boardman do lunch. Champagne, caviar and spaghetti hoops on toast. They are hardly able to contain their laughter at the hilarious way Stan keeps saying 'Germans'.

2.35 p.m. Cilla and Bobby drive through a council estate with their accountant, inwardly laughing at the poor people.

2.55 p.m. Bobby showers using soap-on-a-rope from John Lewis.

3.00 p.m. Graham rings with a quick reminder to see if he's still on the next series.

3.14 p.m. Door bell rings and Cilla hides as Bob Carolgees appears unexpectedly with Spit the Dog.

4.55 p.m. Blind man arrives to re-tune the piano but Cilla mistakes him for a fashion designer and allows him to draw up a collection of outfits for the next series of Blind Date.

5.00 p.m. Bobby rings the Palace again to enquire politely if Cilla's on the next New Year's honours list yet.

6.16 p.m. Ken Dodd, Derek Hatton and Sonya call round for finger buffet and talk of Liverpool and the famous Scouse sense of humour.

11.30 p.m. Evening ends with usual medley of 'Ee You Are A Mucky Kid', 'Alfie', and 'Anyone Who Had A Heart'.

11.55 p.m. Graham rings with a quick reminder that it's bedtime.

TV FACTS 1

In 1987 a little known tribe from the Xingu Reserve, South America, were shown a TV for the first time and were completely fascinated by it until the face of Lesley Joseph appeared. The tribe became very agitated and beat the TV into the ground. Content, they returned happily into the jungle and have never been seen since.

A man in Baguley claimed entry into the **GUINNESS BOOK OF RECORDS** for the continual watching of TV over a period of twelve years non-stop. However, the **GUINNESS BOOK OF RECORDS** disqualified his claim due to the fact he was a known imbecile and had been seen at many bus stops in the area.

Shakespeare often quoted his favourite line 'Forsooth, it bears me ill the sightage of Lesley Joseph's physog on the box.'

The Egyptians actually invented television 4000 years ago but it was a more primitive system involving drawing pictures on the wall.

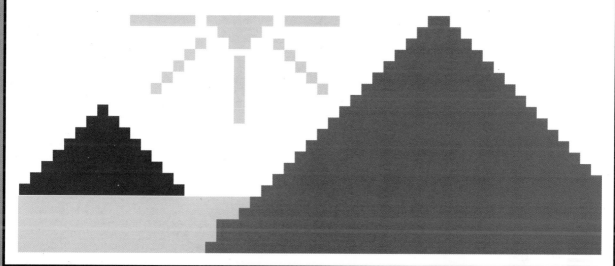

Millions of viewers were fooled into thinking Terry Wogan was a dwarf when he appeared on Children in Need. This was an optical illusion created by the giant-size cheque he was accepting.

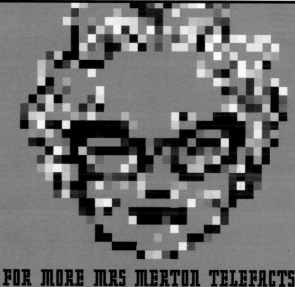

FOR MORE MRS MERTON TELEFACTS
SEE PAGE 110/111

If you laid all the viewers of the Antiques Road Show end-to-end, somebody would have to bear the smell of Lily's feet.

YOUR Views

Dear Mrs Merton

Your show is the best show on the box. That said, I can't abide time travel or science fiction. Who do they think they're fooling? We want more real life on TV, like The Bill and Tenko.

Fay Balmforth
Stafford

Dear Mrs Merton

Where can I buy myself a clock like the one they use on Countdown? I'd also like to know where I can buy a wheel like the one on Wheel of Fortune.

Cal Lavelle
Ward 46, Rampton Hospital

Dear Mrs Merton

Your show is the best show on the box. However, the other day my husband and I were just about to eat our tea (chicken breasts, peas, sweetcorn and boiled potatoes) when without warning I turned Animal Hospital on the telly. A big dog was having a wart removed from what can only be described as his left testicle. Needless to say neither of us felt like the jam roly-poly I'd prepared for pudding.

Jean Cash
Stockport

STAR LETTER

Dear Mrs Merton

I'm thoroughly enjoying reading your book MRS MERTON'S WORLD OF TELEVISION but why don't you include letters from ordinary people like myself on what they think about TV? For instance, I can't stand The Bill.

Maureen Regan
Baguley

Dear Mrs Merton

Has anybody noticed the similarity between the hosts of Pets Win Prizes and Supermarket Sweep? They even share the same name (Dale Winton). Can anyone put me out of my misery on this point?

Peter Kessler
London

Dear Mrs Merton

Robbie Coltrane is a great actor but why is he always cast as a fat man? Surely the casting director could use a bit more imagination. Mind you, he certainly has the figure for it.

Angela Pell
Brighton

PS. Your show is the best show on the box.

Dear Mrs Merton

Just writing to inform you that Angela Lansbury is superb in the role of Jessica Fletcher in the belting series Murder, She Wrote. Yours sincerely,

Angela Lansbury
United States of America

MALCOLM'S Puzzle Page

Which is the plug for the TV?

Join the dots and reveal a mystery household appliance. Can you guess what it is?

2

1

5

WHO AM I ?

I'm your little friend in the corner of the room.
You switch me on to dispel gloom.
I've five channels now and satellite too.
The channel marked 4 is a little bit blue.
You dust me and clean me and treat me with care.
I've been in this corner since Mr Merton had hair.
You've a black and white one of me you keep in the attic.
You can't see a picture, it's too full of static.
What am I, dear reader, have you guessed yet?
Yes, that's right, clever clogs, I'm your TV set!

3

4

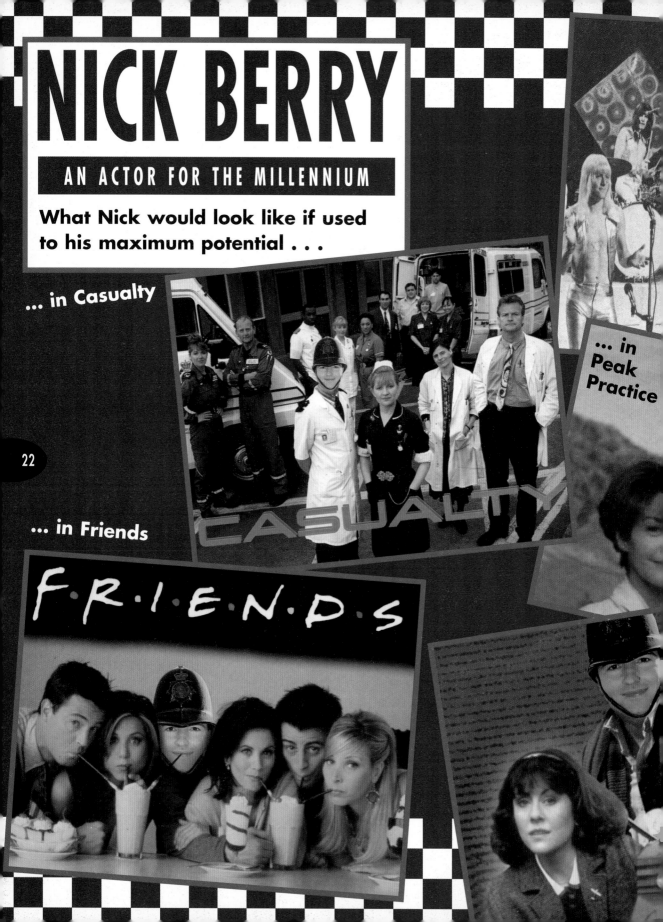

NICK BERRY

AN ACTOR FOR THE MILLENNIUM

What Nick would look like if used to his maximum potential . . .

... in Casualty

... in Peak Practice

... in Friends

... on Top of the Pops

... in London's Burning

... in Baywatch

... in Dr Who

... in The Bill

23

14 Monday

Woke up laughing as I remembered there is a man called Bottom in Shakespeare's 'A Midsummer Night's Dream'
OLD SHAKEY KNEW HOW TO TELL A GOOD REAR-END GAG.
Rang Hollywood to see if there are any parts going for a posh English woman still stuck in the eighteenth century.

15 Tuesday

HAD DICKY FOR LUNCH.
   By which I mean, dear diary, Dicky Attenborough, this time.

Julie Goodyear rang and left a message to see if I could help her get a part in a Merchant Ivory film.
                                 NO WAY!

I RECENTLY FOUND THE DIARY OF EMMA THOMPSON IN HER UNGUARDED HANDBAG. I'M SURE SHE WOULDN'T MIND ME PUBLISHING A WEEK IN THE EXCITING LIFE OF THIS MULTI-TALENTED ACTRESS.

I love Merchant Ivory

16 Wednesday

Woke up in a cold sweat remembering my eighties BBC 2 comedy vehicle 'Thompson'

STAYED IN ALL DAY IN CASE ANYONE ELSE HAD A SIMILAR DREAM.

The Diary of Emma Thompson

Thursday 17

Spent all morning re-writing the works of CHARLES DICKENS.

In the afternoon Vanessas Redgrave, Mae and Feltz came
round for a Vanessa theme party.
Myself and Vanessa (Redgrave) performed some of the
duller scenes from 'Pride and Prejudice',
Vanessa (Mae) accompanied us on the violin,
while Vanessa (Feltz) busied herself in the kitchen.

Friday 18

Tried to ring 'The Big Breakfast' to win a holiday
in Tenerife. COULDN'T GET THROUGH AGAIN!
                    Had candlelit meal with my Oscar.
                    (Fillet steak, medium-rare
                    with bechamel sauce,
                    seasonal vegetables
            and a slice of
                    Walls Vienetta for pud.)

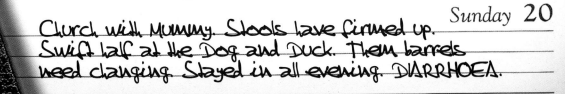

Saturday 19

Stayed in.

DIARRHOEA

Sunday 20

Church with Mummy. Stools have firmed up.
Swift half at the Dog and Duck. Them barrels
need changing. Stayed in all evening. DIARRHOEA.

FILM 47-97 SPECIAL

MRS MERTON

Here's a run down of the top films in the last fifty years:

SISTER ACT

Whoopi Goldberg blacks up yet again, this time to play a comedy nun with hilarious consequences. For my money she's America's answer to Judi Dench.

THE NUN'S STORY

Audrey Hepburn falls in love with Dr Fortunati in the Congo. Luckily for Audrey she was in a select order of make-up wearing nuns.

THE SOUND OF MUSIC

Julie Andrews sings her way through World War II with seven kids dressed in clothes made from curtains. There's a brilliant Eurovision song contest finale and love interest in the shape of a Christopher Plummer lookalike.

NUNS ON THE RUN

Monty Python and ITV's Cracker combine in this hilarious adaption of a true story. They take the fat man/thin man scenario to new clerical heights, especially in the shower scene, never quite fulfilled in over one hundred previous films of the same genre.

SPARTACUS

A marvellous, though sadly nun-free, film that made sandals popular. Marred only by a confusing scene in which many extras claim to be Spartacus. Fortunately the Romans cut a long story short as they know Spartacus is played by Kirk Douglas in one of his many dimple-chinned roles.

THE HEATON NORRIS LOOKALIKE AGENCY

Can't afford a celebrity to open your supermarket? Booking a real celebrity can run into hundreds of pounds (£45.00 for Lesley Joseph) but for just £10.00 you can book each of the following for a full day.

RICHARD AND JUDY

Tony Blair

Sean Connery

SHANE RICHIE

the Spice Girls

Des O'Connor

John Inman

Dale Winton

Richard Branson

David Hasselhoff

29

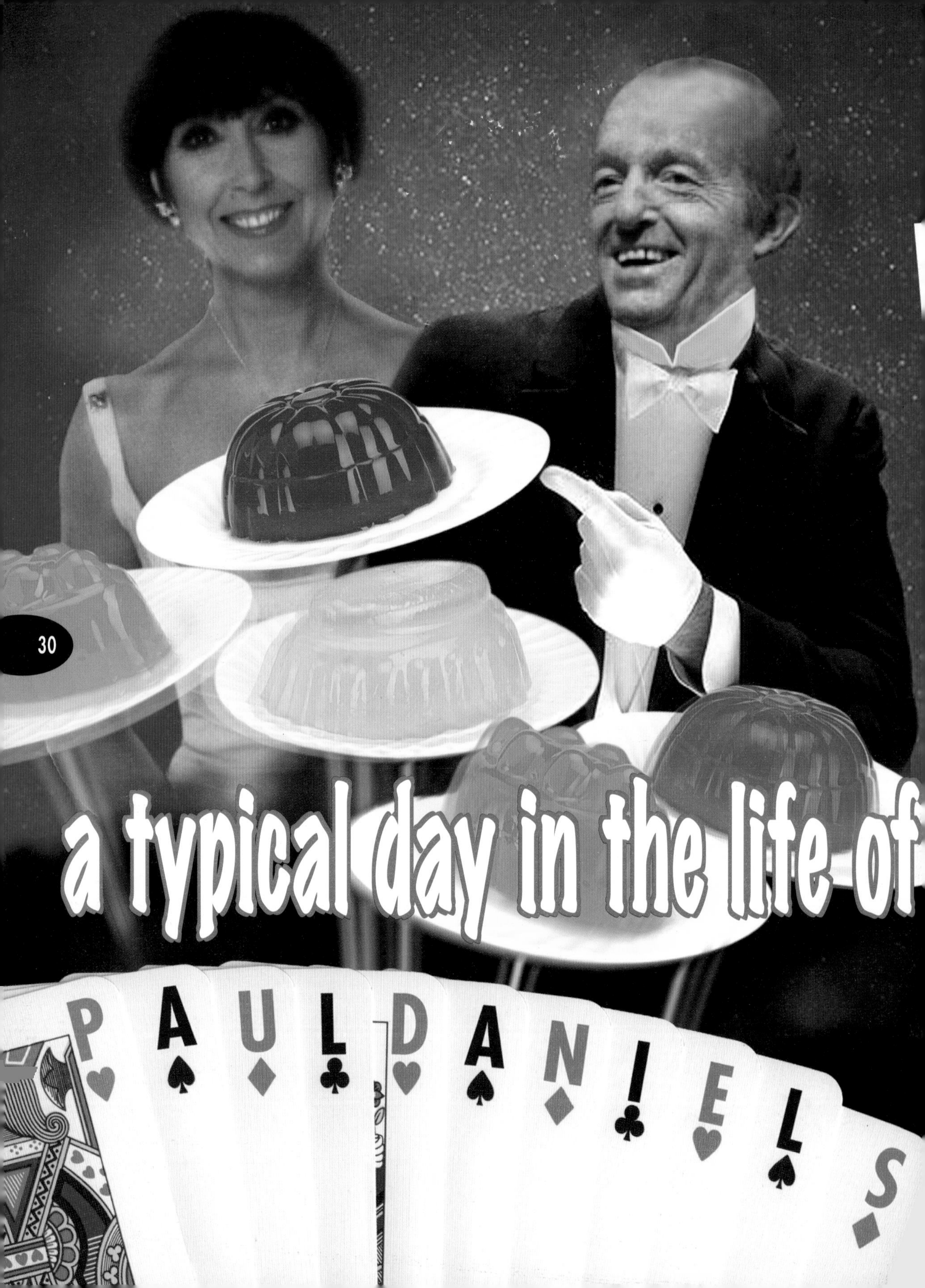

a typical day in the life of

PAUL DANIELS

$4.95

$C5.95/£3.95/FF35
DM15.00/$A12.95/LIT.500
PERIODICALS POSTAGE PAID
USPS 656-960   02371

VARIETY

SUPPLEMENT

10 a.m. Paul wakes up to find he's still grasping his magic wand from the night before. Pulls covers back and several doves fly out.

.30 a.m. Paul goes to Debbie's room but it's locked again.

8.30 a.m. Paul makes breakfast, ably assisted by his wife Debbie, in a striking outfit. Paul does his usual trick with the tea cosy. First there's no tea pot, then there's a tea pot, then there's a boiled egg. Debbie, as usual, is impressed.

11.05 a.m. Paul reads Variety and Stage, checking the obituary columns in both magazines to verify he is still alive and available for work.

12.00 Finishes watching David Copperfield video and wipes his eyes with a towel, attached to a Union Jack, attached to all the flags of the United Nations.

1.15 p.m. Anita Harris pops round for lunch and tries to convince Paul she'd be a better assistant than Debbie. Five costume-changes later, Paul says he's sticking with Debbie. They eat chicken kiev, oven chips and onion rings which are interlocked then independent. For afters they eat jelly off plates spun on poles.

2.45 p.m. Paul tries out his new trick of sawing his beautiful wife Debbie in half lengthways.

4.45 p.m. They return from casualty and Paul rings Anita to see if she can stand in for Debbie for a few weeks.

6.00 p.m. Little Jarvis Cocker pops round for tea and iced fingers. Paul locks him in a coffin with a padlock, puts chains around it and drops it in a swimming pool before Jarvis has the chance to explain that he is not a magician but merely a Brit Pop phenomenon.

7.00 p.m. Dale Winton pops round asking if he can enter Paul's magic circle.

9.15 p.m. Paul sits alone in his room, holding his breath, with a Pot Noodle and some tinned fruit.

11.00 p.m. Showtime. Paul makes his way to the theatre downstairs, where the servants assemble and Paul goes through the show one more time, ably assisted by Anita. In the wings Debbie looks on lovingly through the painkillers.

Mrs Merton's *favourite* TV moments

3 Any appearance of the Irish synchronized dancing sensation Riverdance (post-Michael Flatley).

4 Denis Norden's superb, quick-fire interclip banter in the ever popular It'll Be All Right on the Night series.

1 Where the lovely doctor wife of Nick Berry died in Heartbeat. Luckily there was a sixties pop band on hand to cheer up the proceedings.

2 The National Lottery where I correctly guessed three of the balls, winning myself a tenner.

6 The Eurovision Song Contest when Sir Cliff unveiled his specialized dance routine for 'Power to all our Friends', thus saving his ailing career.

7 Any moment involving Jeremy Beadle dressed up as a traffic warden.

8 That episode of Noel's House Party where an unsuspecting Noel found himself dressed up as the sixth Spice Girl, sporting a comedy beard and tash with hilarious consequences – this time not involving Mr Blobby.

9 Elton John's acting debut as a naughty old gay with a great big wardrobe and a ridiculous wig in the comedy drama Tantrums and Tiaras.

5 When Rita cried so realistically on Coronation Street over the death of her third husband (whose name escapes me – not the one run over by a tram) where real mucus was seemingly coming out of her nostrils. Not many actresses have ever achieved the dual-nostril-mucus cry.

My Winning Numbers

3 **12** **19** **22** **24** **47** **5**

WHAT

they lo

Gin

would

ok like

35

ger?

TVCROSS

36

DOWN

2. Scottish songstress; it sounds like two toilets (4)
3. Knock, knock. Who's there? Doctor (2,3)
4. Chris Tarrant show prior to OTT (6)
5. Bearded buffoon (7)
6. See 18 across (5)
7. What Postman Pat delivers (4)
9. What Prince Charles is in line to the throne, according to Panorama (4)
11. See 6 down (5)
12. On Wheel of Fortune, Jenny Powell is a bit of this (5)
15. Chris Tarrant show, after Tiswas (1,1,1)
16. News at … Also Malcolm's bed-time and title of a film starring Bo Derek (3)
17. Big-breasted star of film 10, not Dudley (2)

ACROSS

1. Game show where contestants win a blind date thanks to Cilla (5,4)
5. Billy, brother of Wheel of Fortune's Bradley (5,5)
6. Close friends get to call him T.C. (3,3)
8. One half of the hilarious double act Hinge and Bracket (5)
10. Ian St. John's middle name (2)
13. We've all seen this O'Mara's triangle on TV (4)
14. Irish lottery, or Lotto as the Irish call it (5)
17. Does this Cheryl hang around with a butcher and a candlestick maker? (5)
18. Drama series of women in popular Japanese prisoner-of-war camp (5)

ANSWERS
ACROSS
1. BLIND DATE. 5. BILLY WALSH. 6. TOP CAT. 8. HINGE. 10. ST. 13. KATE.
14. LOTTO. 17. BAKER. 18. TENKO.
DOWN
2. LULU. 3. DR WHO. 4. TISWAS. 5. BUSHELL. 6. TENKO. 7. POST.
9. NEXT. 11. TENKO. 12. SKIRT. 15. OTT. 16. TEN. 17. BO.

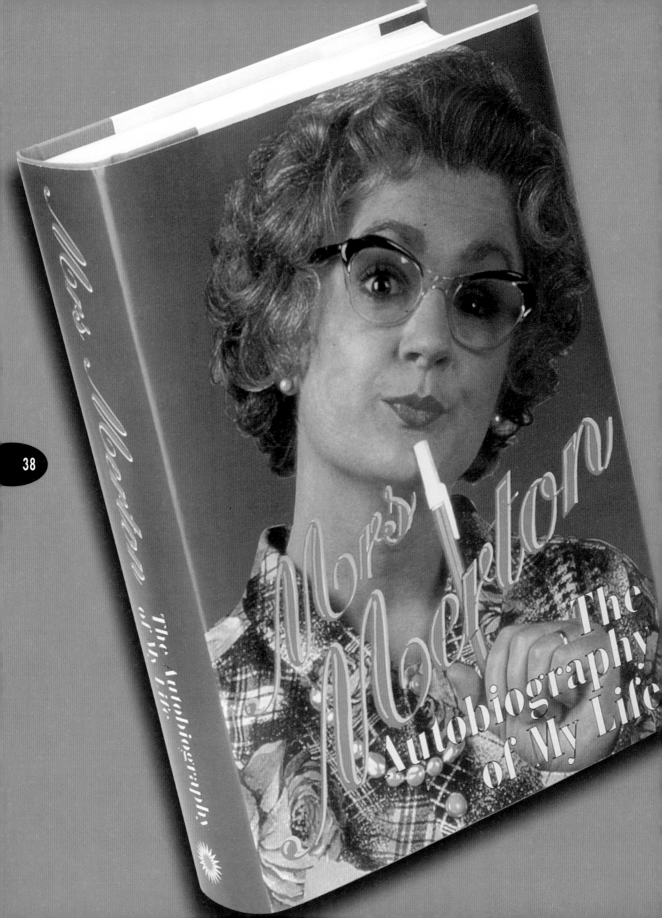

Mrs Merton

Mrs Merton

The Autobiography of My Life

The Autobiography of My Life

How An Ordinary, Well-Informed Lady Got Into TV

'There's nothing on TV again,' sighed Mr Merton, my husband, one Christmas day as Lesley Joseph's face filled the screen. 'You could do better than that Mrs Merton,' exclaimed Mr Merton.

'Yes, Mam,' agreed Malcolm Merton, my son, looking up from his sponge painting.

I decided to ring the BBC again and complain. The phone was answered by a young man called Alan Yentob. We had a right good chin wag until I realized it was on our bill. 'Call me back Al, my ol' mate,' I said.

'Better than that,' he said, 'I'll nip round to Heaton Norris.' I barely had time to cut the Battenburg before an over-excited, besuited, bearded, balding man was on the doorstep. 'Come on in old Yentob-head,' I said, and we carried on our conversation from where we'd left off, with him slagging off all the right people for a good twenty minutes. 'You should be head of BBC 1,' I said.

'I am, ' replied Alan Yentob, whereupon I immediately offered him another piece of Battenburg.

Malcolm realized it was time for jim-jams but asked if he could share a fudge finger with Alan before bed.

'You should have your own programme, Mrs Merton,' said Yentob.

We all laughed, while Alan helped himself to another slice of Battenburg.

10 THINGS YOU DIDN'T KNOW ABOUT
Lesley Joseph

1. She's an actress.

2. Both her first and last names could be boys' names.

3. She plays the third most popular character in TV's Birds of a Feather.

4. There is still plenty of mileage in the ruse that she is a man-mad siren.

5. She is younger than Barbara Cartland.

6. She allegedly lights her own trumps at parties.

7 Her name in Latin means mutton dressed as lamb.

8 As a girl even her imaginary friends didn't want to know her.

9 My friend Lily swears blind that she is a seventy-eight year old man.

10 She shares her initials with

BLIND Celebrity DATE

Over the page we've got three lovely celebrity lads.
You can choose one of them.
To help you decide we've got your three questions.

Question 1
I'm like a kitten . . . soft and playful.
If you were an animal what would you be?

Number 3 I'm also like a cat. A cat on a hot tin roof. And if you were a hot tin roof I wouldn't want to get off you.

Number 2 I'm also a cat. But I'm the Cat in the Hat. If you were a hat then wherever I laid you would be my home.

Number 1 I'm also like a cat, but I'm a tom cat. I'll be your Tom if you'll be my Jerry . . . by which I don't mean German.

Question 2
I love water sports. What sport do you love?

Number 1 Boxing . . . wrestling. I like anything in the ring.

Number 2 My favourite sport is the *Sunday Sport* because I like looking at naked girls with big busters and, to be quite honest, I wouldn't mind a sporty go on yours.

Number 3 *(recites a poem)* I like skiing and I like drinking too, So I'd like nothing more than to be on the piste with you.

Question 3
I'm often complimented on my legs. What do you think is the best bit of you?

Number 1 I'd have to go for my bottom. Most people do.

Number 3 When I'm wearing lycra there is one thing that stands out . . . My right thigh.

Number 2 My penis.

DON'T CHOOSE YET
. . . here's our Graham
with a quick reminder

Will you choose Number 1, who's a cat with a nice bottom who's boxing clever for you? Or will it be Number 2, who's a cat with a penis – but girls, watch those busters, because that's what he'll be after? Or will it be poetic Number 3, who's a cat who likes his right thigh and dreadful puns?
The choice is yours . . .

Turn the page to reveal the contestants . . .

You've picked a big hunk . . .

1 DALE WINTON

2 PIERCE BROSNAN

3 MR MOTIVATOR

44

. . . *but* *look at the two you've turned down*

Having witnessed first hand my successful venture into showbusiness my only son Malcolm Merton decided he fancied a taste of the greasepaint, and after only two years on the waiting list, he joyfully accepted a major role as an extra on Cracker, the plump detective show starring Robbie Coltrane in the title role.

When we arrived on the set they informed us that Malcolm was to play a dead body brought out of the morgue with a tag tied to his toe. After much argument between myself and the director, as to which toe was to be tagged, we reached a compromise (big toe, left foot). Malcolm finds it difficult to speak up for himself on these occasions and I think he was glad I'd stuck up for him. Later I asked Mr Coltrane what he thought of Malcolm's performance. He was 100% on my side, saying that he thought it was a nice twist that Malcolm was allowed to be on the slab with his recorder beside him, even though the director had thought it irrelevant to the plot and confusing to the viewer.

Although the scene was cut due to more alcohol consumption scenes being inserted with the portly star, it hasn't discouraged Malcolm from adamantly pointing out every dead body on Wycliffe or Ruth Rendell and explaining how it should have been played.

45

THE DAY I MET
KEVIN COSTNER
AND
RICHARD WHITELEY

IT WAS THE 16 JUNE 1992. My son, Malcolm Merton, had heard that a circus was in town and I had procured tickets ringside as a special treat. In the interval Malcolm popped off for a Kia Ora, only to come back breathless and obviously excited, saying that he had seen Kevin Costner licking a Cornetto outside the mens' toilets.

'It must be a lookey-likey,' I said to Malcolm, having myself just seen Richard Whiteley – or at least a lookey-likey Whiteley – and realizing the improbability of seeing two showbiz legends under the same Big Top.

At that point a trio of clowns came on with a bucket of what we supposed to be water, but which we found out later to our hilarity, only contained confetti. My attention began to wane when an elderly trapeze artist entered the ring and I found myself looking for further lookey-likeys.

Later that same week, when watching Countdown I noticed that Kevin Costner was the celebrity in Dictionary Corner, and realized they must be chums with a shared passion for circuses. I wondered if their interest had waned during the elderly-trapeze-artist-act and if they had recognized me and thought me a lookey-likey. We will never know . . .

4

BBC SITUATIONS VACANT

DON'T WANT TO BOTHER WITH EXPENSIVE CANNED LAUGHTER.

Call Chris Akabusi any time, night or day.

Looking for a floppy-fringed Hugh Grant type?

Try Hugh Grant on 0898 10

ACTOR SEEKS WORK.

YOUNG BOY GOING THROUGH A DIFFICULT STAGE. ONE-FOOTED GRANDFATHER A SPECIALITY.

CALL NICKY PLATT

I CAN PLAY A POSH LADY TO ANY MANOR BORN

There's only one Penelope Keith and it's me.

Ring Penny on Hampshire 432 567

NEED AN OLD ACTRESS WHO'LL STILL GET HER BAPS OUT?

CALL HELEN MIRREN ON 0171 345 34

Need an ugly Geordie to kiss attractive women in self-penned scripts?

You can't fail, call Jimmy Nail 0191 325 016

Is your show feeling tired and listless? Need a rotund stargazer to lift it up?

CALL RUSSELL GRANT.

ROBSON AND JEROME
available for work.

(Will separate.)

WANT FRANK SPENCER? WANT RONNIE CORBETT? WANT HAROLD WILSON?

TOO EXPENSIVE?

TRY ME, STEVE COOGAN.
CALL 0171 882 30??
(NO TIME WASTERS

Does your show need
a Hylda Baker impression?

Faith Brown's your man.
CALL NOW !

HELENA BONHAM-CARTER
NOT AVAILABLE?
_____

Try
CATHERINE ZETA-JONES
for all your
double-barrelled needs.

Popular actress
LESLEY JOSEPH seeks work
in foreign locations
for next five years.

Contact:
LINDA ROBSON
or PAULINE QUIRKE.
345 7685

Need Jesus of Nazareth lookalike
with fish-faced side-kick?
No role too embarrassing.
Call
Robert Powell 0181 4

SWEDISH BLONDE
will do anything on television
~~within~~ reason.
Ring
ULRIKA JONSSON - 0898 5?

LOWEST COMMON
DENOMINATOR NOT
CATERED FOR ?
You need bearded Noel Edmonds.
(Own Gunge tank.) Call 0171 435

THE PAUL McKENNA
HYPNOTISING
MASK

The hypnotist Paul McKenna has secured a highly lucrative contract with ITV although none of the ITV bosses have any memory of the event. This power can now be yours with the Paul McKenna hypnotising mask.

How to use:
1. Cut along dotted line
2. Tie mask over face with string
3. Ask subject to look into your eyes
4. Command subject to do your bidding

51

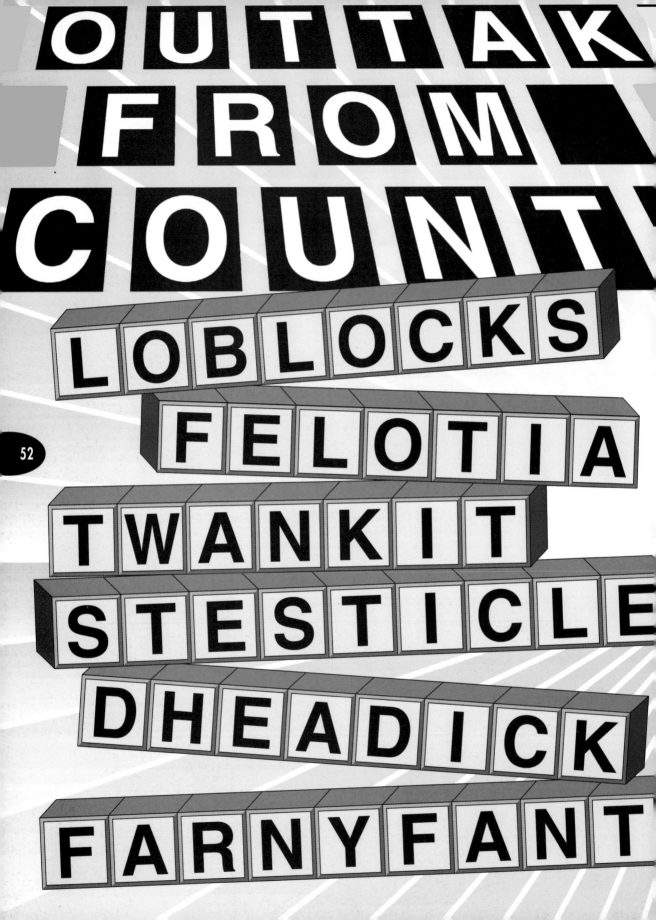

OUTTAK
FROM
COUNT

LOBLOCKS
FELOTIA
TWANKIT
STESTICLE
DHEADICK
FARNYFANT

52

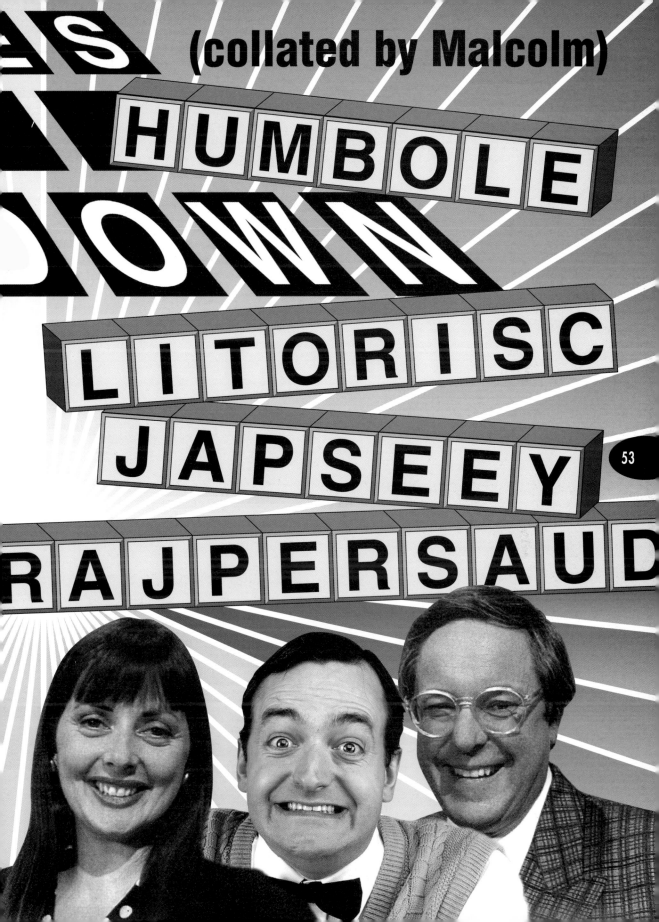

Popular Rumours

all rumours started by my friend Lily

54

PAUL WHITEHOUSE was so delighted with the first series of The Fast Show that he slept with his writing partner Charlie Higson and ordered champagne and kiwi fruit from room service at a popular London hotel.

ANTHEA TURNER has never revealed to her family that she works in television. To this day they are proud of Anthea – the legal secretary.

There is no such planet as URANUS. It was invented by a research working on The Sky a Night in order to humiliate **PATRICK MOORE.**

RINGO STARR read the *Thomas the Tank Engine* stories as a favour to its inventor Reverend W. H. Aubrey who drummed on 'I Want to Hold Your Hand' in 1963.

CHRIS EUBANK uses a spirit level to keep the top of his head flat.

GEORGE BEST is a Siamese twin. The brother also called George played on the right wing fo Manchester United but fo some reason was never recognized and faded into obscurity.

The well-known film critic **BARRY NORMAN** often visits his local cinema and shouts out the endings to films thus spoiling it for the rest of the cinema-going public.

LITTLE AND LARGE arm-wrestle before every show to decide who will be the straight man that night. For many years they have had to settle for a draw.

DAVE LEE TRAVIS' brother, Barry, invented the BL sandwich.

LISA STANSFIELD has a huge collection of coat hangers that she conceals beneath the huge collection of clothing in her wardrobe.

In his spare time **JIMMY TARBUCK** sets up a stall at various local fairs and does face painting for children.

PETER SISSONS keeps calm whilst reading the news by dangling his two testicles in a tropical fish tank concealed beneath his desk.

When you receive a Gratton's catalogue, Scottish songstress **LULU** comes round in person to take your first order. (Orders over £15.00 only.)

STEVE COOGAN often invites members of his fan club round to his luxury apartment where he treats them to vol-au-vents and rare video footage of his first holy communion directed by a very young Patrick Marber.

Whenever **BRUCE WILLIS** is in the UK, he makes a point of watching daytime game-show Chain Letters hosted by Bolton funny-man Dave Spikey.

RICHARD BRANSON often visits London's homeless and hands out free promotional copies of Mike Oldfield's 'Tubular Bells'.

10
THINGS YOU DIDN'T KNOW ABOUT
Ulrika Jonsson

1 *Ulrika's skin is real.*

2 *She lives in a spacious four-bedroom sauna.*

3 *As a child she never wore clothes until the age of 18 and was very popular at school, especially during gym class.*

4 *She once borrowed Mick Hucknall's ruby tooth for a ball in Sweden.*

5 *Her ambition is to be one of the original Brontë sisters.*

6 *She has never appeared in public.*

7 *Scientists have refused to accept her brain after she dies.*

8 *Since 1991 she has refused to eat food out of public bins and waste disposal units.*

9 *She is the voice of Graham with a quick reminder on Blind Date.*

10 *She learnt to spell 'necessary' by using the following sentence: 'Never Eat Chocolate, Eat Salad Sandwiches And Remain Young.'*

What the stars are really like!

Bridie tells all

For years a friend of mine, Bridie, worked in the BBC Canteen serving celebrities with their dinners, puddings and beverages. After being made redundant due to reaching pensionable age she can no longer maintain her silence and has talked exclusively to me and my friend Lily in the doctor's waiting room.

BBC

Name of Holder: ~~Mr.Mrs.~~Miss ~~Ms~~

BRIDIE WINTERTON

AJG 2322

BBC 3588/

Bridie says …

Rosemary is always on TV going on about dieting and slimming and losing weight. Yet when she came into my canteen I'm sure I overheard her say 'I could eat a scabby dog.' She then proceeded to eat the following: 2 portions of chips, egg, sausage, bacon, beans, 2 slices of fried bread, tomatoes, black pudding, 4 slices of bread and butter (thick-sliced) and finished it off with sticky toffee pudding and a can of Cola (not diet). This would have to happen on a day when I wasn't wearing my glasses and couldn't swear for sure it was Rosemary Conley. It was certainly some greedy pig in a leotard.

Bridie says …
Mr Grossman claims to love his food. Well, I know different! He came into my canteen once and ordered steak and kidney pie, new potatoes and green beans. Whilst he ate the new potatoes and the green beans he hardly touched his pie, and wasn't in the least bit interested in any of the apple crumble. It just goes to show – you can't believe everything you see on TV!

Bridie says …
I'd always thought this man was the model of politeness and charm but I was shocked to the core when in 1987 he tried to pass off an Irish 10p as legal tender in my canteen.

Bridie says …
Shane is the nicest man in show business. He came into my canteen once and kissed me on the cheek, kissed Janice on the till, and then performed a ten-minute stand-up routine with a sausage. He then happily posed for photos and had even brought his own camera. And to think he was passing by and wasn't even working at the BBC that day!
A true star!!

Bridie says …
Mr Edmonds is a filthy old bearded man. I overheard him offering two of the trainee canteen staff a look at his chopper in the field at the back of the BBC!

59

MY IDEAL MAN

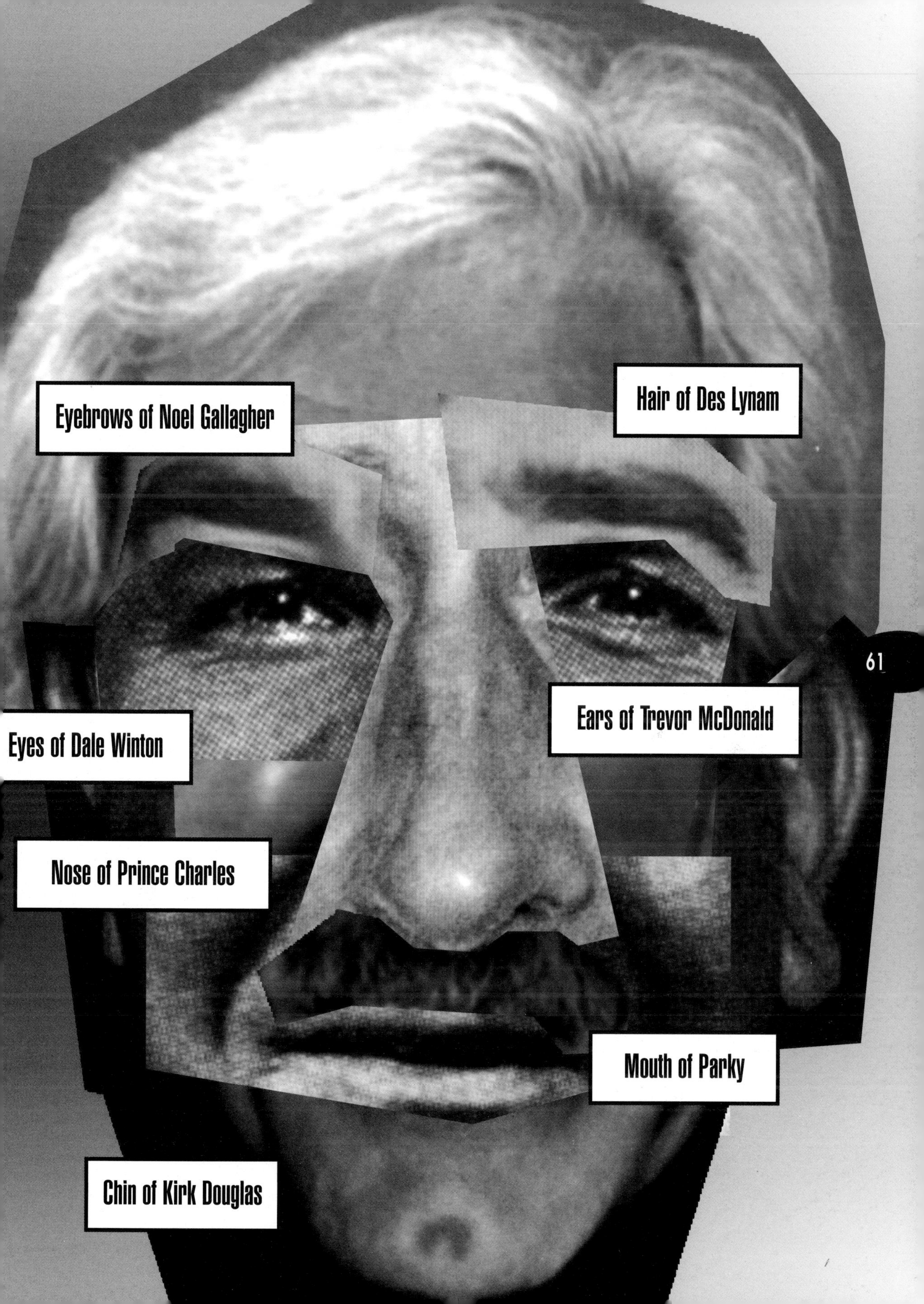

Eyebrows of Noel Gallagher

Hair of Des Lynam

Eyes of Dale Winton

Ears of Trevor McDonald

Nose of Prince Charles

Mouth of Parky

Chin of Kirk Douglas

TV COPS

NAME	Jane Tennison, Prime Suspect
LOCATION	Manchester & London
FORMAT	Hard-faced Helen Mirren type.
FLAW	Can't hold down a steady boyfriend and has to make do with one-night stands involving peripheral characters.
CATCHPHRASE	'I don't have to show my boobies in this programme, I'm a police woman.'
EXTRA INFORMATION	Constantly taken off the case for being a woman then re-instated as she always knows who the killer is - usually the Prime Suspect as the title suggested all along.

100%

SUCCESS RATE AT CATCHING CRIMINALS

NAME	Kojak
LOCATION	New York
FORMAT	Seventies costume drama with bald-headed man and curly-haired real-life brother.
FLAW	Viewers were often confused as to which was the lolly and which was his head.
CATCHPHRASE	'Stop licking my head.'
EXTRA INFORMATION	Duncan Goodhew auditioned for this role.

SUCCESS RATE AT CATCHING CRIMINALS 100%

NAME	Inspector Frost
LOCATION	Leeds
FORMAT	Caring 'Del Boy' look-a-like detective.
FLAW	None of the replacements for Rodney are as funny.
CATCHPHRASE	'You're wicked. Lovely jubbley!'
EXTRA INFORMATION	The episode where Ronnie Barker appeared as a stuttering shopkeeper was hilarious.

SUCCESS RATE AT CATCHING CRIMINALS 100%

NAME	SPENDER
LOCATION	NORTH-EAST
FORMAT	EX-BRICKLAYER AND JIMMY NAIL LOOKALIKE TURNED POLICEMAN.
FLAW	HIS COVER WAS BLOWN WHEN HE APPEARED ON TOP OF THE POPS.
CATCHPHRASE	'SHE'S LYING.'
EXTRA INFORMATION	THREW A PADDY WHEN HE WASN'T ALLOWED TO PLAY EVERY PART.

100%

SUCCESS RATE AT CATCHING CRIMINALS

NAME	Ironside
LOCATION	U.S.A.
FORMAT	Minority-interest detective.
FLAW	Not so fast at chasing criminals uphill.
CATCHPHRASE	'Uh oh, stairs!'
EXTRA INFORMATION	Still remains the most popular wheelchair detective.

100%

SUCCESS RATE AT CATCHING CRIMINALS

NAME	Cagney and Lacey
LOCATION	New York
FORMAT	Solving crime on the change.
FLAW	They really want to be on a cookery programme.
CATCHPHRASE	'Shall I go to my son's school play or shall I stake out a drug-dealing pimp?'
EXTRA INFORMATION	Authentic use of eighties costumes and settings.

SUCCESS RATE AT CATCHING CRIMINALS

100%

NAME	Inspector Morse
LOCATION	Oxford
FORMAT	Crime solved by a big, close-up on John Thaw's face.
FLAW	Only seems to be bothered about deaths of posh people.
CATCHPHRASE	'There's no rush, stick on a bit of opera.'
EXTRA INFORMATION	Nearly married Thora Hird, but she didn't want to become Thora Thaw.

100%

SUCCESS RATE AT CATCHING CRIMINALS

The Day I Met Andi Peters

I had absolutely no idea that my son, Malcolm Merton, and my husband, Mr Merton, were planning anything for my birthday. I had got dressed up purely on the off-chance and to be quite honest, I had seen Mr Merton collecting 'buy one, get one free' coupons from Pizza Hut. When they announced they were taking me to Pizza Hut, I was completely surprised and delighted. I had only recently started getting a taste for foreign food and pizza was up there with pasta on the Italian side of things.

We were sitting happily in the restaurant and the waitress was explaining to Malcolm how they bake the cheese into the crust, when who should appear from the toilets but little Andi Peters, the bubbly children's TV presenter. All thoughts of cheesy crust went out the window as Malcolm recognized his screen hero, helping himself at the all-you-can-eat salad bar.

'I want salad now, Mam,' shouted Malcolm. I knew this was a ruse as earlier he had no interest in side-dishes of any nature. Malcolm skipped off to meet his hero. A few minutes later, a jubilant Malcolm returned, clutching an empty bowl which in the

excitement he'd forgotten to fill.

'What did he say?' I asked Malcolm.

'He said that he likes coleslaw but he couldn't stand red kidney beans.' Malcolm could hardly contain himself. 'It feels like my birthday too now.'

Thank you Andi Peters, whoever you are.

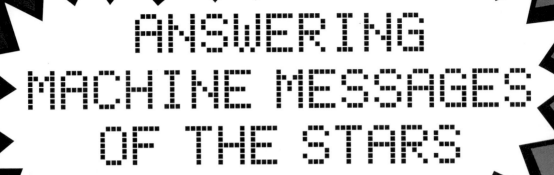

ANSWERING MACHINE MESSAGES OF THE STARS

A'wight . . .
this is Michael Barrymore.
I'm out at the moment . . .
until public interest dies down.

Ooh Betty, the cat's done a whoopsy!
Ooh Everard, shut that door, like I said to
my wife Mary at the Blackpool conference . . .
This is Steve Coogan and, yes, I'll do anything.

Hello, this is Cilla, please leave a message after the tone
- but first, here's Graham with a quick reminder.
Hello, Graham here, leave a message for Cilla after the tone ...

G'day, this is Kylie Minogue,
I'm afraid I'm not in at the moment
... but that's fashion.

69

Hello, I'm not in at the minute
... Yes I am! It's me,
TV prankster Jeremy Beadle.
Leave a message after the tone
(BEEP). Ha ha ha.
That's not it, fooled you ...
it's the next tone (BEEP)
or is it the tone after that!
Ah ah ah, you can never tell
with me (BEEP) ...

Hello (BONG), this is
Trevor McDonald
(BONG). Please
leave a message after
the bong (BONG).

CELEBRITY LOTTERY

MAKES WINNING A LITTLE MORE FUN

Here are forty-nine celebrities with their lucky numbers.
Choose your favourite six celebrities and play them as your lottery
numbers each week. See if your favourite celebrities can bring you luck.
For example if your favourite celebrities are Oliver Reed, Terry
Christian, Jenny Powell, Patsy Kensit, Nigel Havers and Kiki Dee,
then your numbers are 1, 15, 17, 27, 42, 46.

 1 Oliver Reed

 2 Sarah Brightman

 3 Andi Peters

 4 Matthew Kelly

 5 Paul Gascoigne

 6 Zeinab Badawi

 7 Paul Gambaccini

 Dec 8

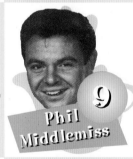 9 Phil Middlemiss

 10 Lorraine Kelly

 11 Lenny Henry

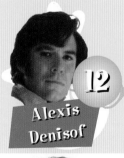 12 Alexis Denisof

 13 Carol Smillie

 14 David Baddiel

 15 Terry Christian

 16 Alan Titchmarsh

 17 Jenny Powell

 18 Jilly Goolden

 19 Danny Baker

 20 Eamonn Holmes

21 Paul McKenna

22 Zig

23 Ned Sherrin

24 Geri (Ginger Spice)

25 Big Daddy

26 Roland Rat

27 Patsy Kensit

28 Stephanie Beacham

29 Bonehead (Oasis)

30 Ernie Wise

31 Hugh Scully

32 Peter Purves

33 Art Malik

34 William Shatner

35 Lulu

71

36 Wolf

37 Jeremy Irons

38 Boris Becker

39 William Roache

40 Ainsley Harriott

41 Zoë Ball

42 Nigel Havers

43 Janet Street-Porter

44 Joan Collins

45 Ben Elton

46 Kiki Dee

47 Emma Forbes

48 Nanette Newman

49 Bobby Ball

IT'S AS EASY AS THAT!

Open and close book on this page
and witness the sultry Des Lynam
stealing a kiss on my lips.

72

73

A TYPICAL DAY IN THE LIFE OF

Hugh SCULLY

7.30 A.M.   WAKES UP IN A VICTORIAN FOUR-POSTER BED, CIRCA 1872, IN A DELIGHTFUL ENGLISH MARKET TOWN.

8.00 A.M.   OPENS WINDOWS TO SEE HARRY SECOMBE SINGING ON A NEARBY GRASS VERGE OPPOSITE AN OLD CHURCH.

9.30 A.M.   BREAKFAST WITH J. R. HARTLEY ON ROYAL DOULTON CHINA FROM JOHN LEWIS'S. THEY EAT STEWED PRUNES AND KIPPERS IN A BASKET.

10.40 AM   MR KIPLING COMES BY WITH SOME BRAMLEY APPLE SLICES WITH TWO RUDDY-CHEEKED YOUNG CHAPS IN TOW. 'YOU GET MORE FOR A PAIR,' SAYS HUGH JOKING.

12.00   HUGH LUNCHES ON A PINE IKEA TABLE WITH PETER USTINOV, NED SHERRIN AND FAITH BROWN. THEY SHARE A 200-YEAR-OLD CLARET AND A FAMILY-SIZED BAG OF CHEESY WOTSITS.

1.00 P.M.   HUGH GOES OUT FOR A RIDE IN THE ENGLISH COUNTRYSIDE ON HIS PENNY FARTHING AND STOPS FOR CLOTTED CREAM WITH A CLOSE NEIGHBOUR, BETTY. BETTY ASKS HIM TO EXAMINE WHAT SHE BELIEVES TO BE POSSIBLE ANTIQUE FRIDGE MAGNETS. HUGH POINTS OUT THAT OSCAR® WINNERS WALLACE AND GROMIT WEREN'T INVENTED UNTIL THE LATTER HALF OF THIS CENTURY.

4.45 P.M.   HUGH RETURNS HIS BOOKS TO THE LOCAL LIBRARY. ONE IS *STAINED GLASS IN THE FIFTEENTH CENTURY* AND THE OTHER *MICROWAVE MEALS FOR ONE*. THE ELDERLY LIBRARIAN SHOWS HUGH A PLATE WHICH SHE BELIEVES DEPICTS QUEEN ANNE BUT HUGH POINTS OUT THAT IT IS IN FACT PRINCESS ANNE, HENCE THE PICTURE OF CAPTAIN MARK PHILLIPS BY HER SIDE.

5.30 P.M.   HUGH GOES TO BED WITH A TOBY JUG OF COCOA AND A TUPPERWARE BOWL OF QUAVERS. HE FALLS ASLEEP QUICKLY BUT AWAKENS AT 9.30 P.M. TO FIND IRRITATING QUAVER CRUMBS IN HIS BELLY BUTTON.

77

Colour by NUMBERS

Richard and Judy

Barbara Cartland

| 1 | 2 | 3 |

10 things you didn't know about

1. He wears a mask in public.
No-one really knows what he looks like.

2. In 1991 he auditioned for the role of little orphan Annie but was pipped at the post by an unknown child actress.

3. He is thought to be Chinese from the waist down.

4. He is best friends with Andi Peters and Delia Smith.

5. He has appeared on University Challenge more times that anyone except Bamber Gascoigne.

6. His pastimes include karaoke and keyhole surgery.

7. He refuses point blank to eat anything poisonous.

8. He is a big fan of canned laughter.

Jeremy

Paxman

9 He can't say the word 'chestnut'.

10 He often appears as an extra in Emmerdale.

HOW YOUR LICENCE FEE IS SPENT

Every pound you spend on the licence fee is spent like this

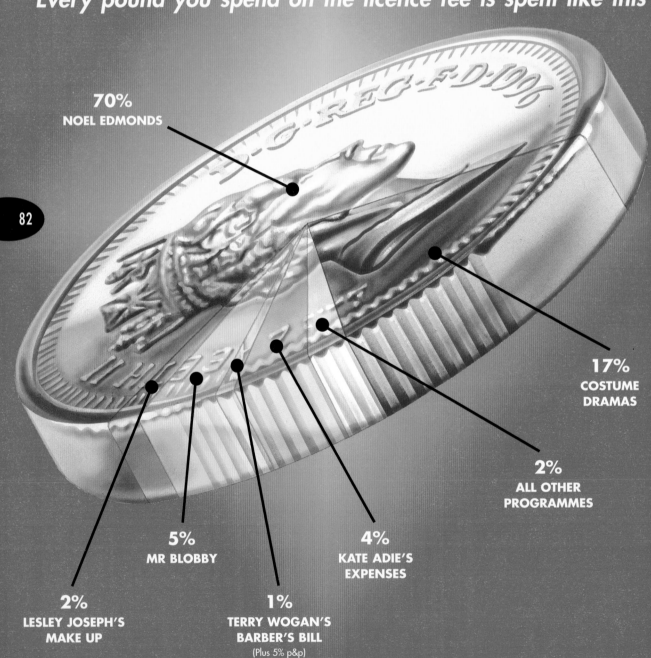

70%
NOEL EDMONDS

17%
COSTUME
DRAMAS

2%
ALL OTHER
PROGRAMMES

5%
MR BLOBBY

4%
KATE ADIE'S
EXPENSES

2%
LESLEY JOSEPH'S
MAKE UP

1%
TERRY WOGAN'S
BARBER'S BILL
(Plus 5% p&p)

HOW MUCH DO YOUR FAVOURITE CELEBRITIES EARN?

JUDY FINNIGAN
£1.5 MILLION

RICHARD MADELEY
£1.4 MILLION

SHANE RICHIE
£40 A WEEK FROM THE GOVERNMENT
(on enterprise allowance scheme as trainee tv presenter)

ANGELA LANSBURY
18P PER WORD

DELIA SMITH
£100 PER SHOW
(and all she can eat)

CAROL VORDERMAN
£29 MILLION

ZIG AND ZAG
£17 MILLION

ALAN TITCHMARCH
£2 MILLION

QUEEN ELIZABETH II
£2 MILLION PER SHOW
(Which is why BBC and ITV can only afford a Christmas special)

MRS MERTON
UNKNOWN
(but is thought to be all donated to charity)

Daniel O'Donnel

SEWING PATTERN

Now you can have Daniel O'Donnel's head on your pillow. Make your dreams come true with a darning needle and a two-pound ball of mixed wool

· HERE'S HOW TO DO IT ·

1. Align pattern with pillow.

2. Follow line of pattern with wool.

3. Lay your head next to Daniel's and rest easy...

FAMOUS TV FAMILY TREES

THE GASCOIGNE FAMILY

BAMBER GASCOIGNE

JILL GASCOINE

PAUL GASCOIGNE

THE SIMON FAMILY

PAUL SIMON

CARLY SIMON

SIMPLE SIMON

THE ROSS FAMILY

NICK ROSS

DIANA ROSS

JONATHAN ROSS

THE DIAMOND FAMILY

NEIL DIAMOND

ANNE DIAMOND

DOUBLE DIAMOND

JIM DIAMOND

A DIAMOND

THE EVANS FAMILY

DEREK EVANS
(MR MOTIVATOR)

LINDA EVANS

CHRIS EVANS

87

THE BEHR FAMILY

DANI BEHR

HUGGY BEHR

YOGI BEHR

POOH BEHR

THE WRIGHT BROTHERS

STEVE WRIGHT

IAN WRIGHT

THE MOORE FAMILY

PATRICK MOORE

BRIAN MOORE

ROGER MOORE

DEMI MOORE

THE BAKER FAMILY

DANNY BAKER

CHERYL BAKER

TOM BAKER

COLIN BAKER

88

THE GRANT FAMILY

RUSSELL GRANT

HUGH GRANT

RICHARD E. GRANT

EDDIE GRANT

THE O'CONNOR FAMILY

HAZEL O'CONNOR

TOM O'CONNOR

DES O'CONNOR

SINEAD O'CONNOR

THE FINNIGAN FAMILY

JUDY FINNIGAN

MICHAEL FINNIGAN
(HE GREW WHISKERS ON
HIS CHINNIGAN)

THE FOX FAMILY

EDWARD FOX

SAM FOX

BASIL BRUSH

THE FISH FAMILY

MICHAEL FISH

A FISH

FISH (FROM MARILLION)

the day I met Richard Branson

'The sun's very orange today,' said Malcolm Merton, my son, looking out of his boxroom window.

'That's not the sun,' I said. 'That's a hot air balloon.'

'Who could that possibly be?' asked Malcolm.

'Whoever that bearded person is, they're landing in our garden,' I cried.

Immediately, I put the kettle on and Malcolm set about slicing a date and walnut cake. Whoever it was landing in my back garden would surely be in need of refreshment at this time of the afternoon. We opened the back door to see the balloon lodged in our back hedge and a bearded entrepreneur smiling sheepishly by the side.

'Don't worry about the damage, Mrs Merton,' he said, 'I'm worth a few bob.'

Hours later, myself, the bearded entrepreneur and Malcolm were enjoying a game of Happy Families when the door bell rang.

'That'll be for me,' said the stranger. A tall posh chauffeur was standing there and said, 'Are you ready, Mr Richard Branson?' Myself and Malcolm exchanged completely puzzled glances, then gradually the dawning of an idea came to Malcolm.

'Hang on, Mam,' said Malcolm, turning to the stranger. 'Balloon, beard, entrepreneur, Virgin T-shirt – you're not that Richard Branson, the bearded Virgin entrepreneur balloonist?'

'Yes, Malcolm Merton,' said Richard, and with that he thrust a shiny fifty-pence coin into my son's hand. 'I'll never forget your kindness,' he said taking the last slice of the date and walnut cake and heading off into the night.

Two days later I received a huge, exciting-looking parcel through the post. It was a thank-you gift from Richard Branson and it contained a dozen cans of Virgin Cola, a copy of Mike Oldfield's 'Tubular Bells' and a large stamped addressed envelope for the return of his balloon.

Needless to say, I binned 'Tubular Bells.'

91

A Friend of Mine, Lily's, Autograph Book

By hook or by crook I'll be first in this book

Desmond Tutu

Lily says... I didn't know who he was at the time but later Channel 4 made a documentary about his barber shop, called Desmond's.

Mr. Derele Motivator

Lily says... Obtained this autograph while he was jogging. Took me four and a half miles.

Remember me ?
Dave Lee Travis
DLT, the Hairy Cornflake

Lily says... I didn't ask for this but I was sedated in hospital at the time. He was the hospital radio DJ and had snuck into my ward.

Eddie Large

Lily says... Who'd have thought that these TV funsters' autographs would be in such contrast to their stage personas? Proof, if proof were needed, that they're just as hilarious off stage as on.

Syd Littl

Carol Vorderman

Richard Whiteley

Lily says... I got these in Majorca where they were having a well-deserved break from vowels and consonants.

andi peters

I'm Simply the Best Steve Coogan.

Lily says... I have no idea who this children's TV presenter is.

Lily says... Steve was lovely, and insisted on going through his full repertoire from Frank Spencer to Charlie Drake. As we were in the precinct at the time he gathered quite a crowd, and when he passed the hat round he made £27.00.

Sir Cliff Richard

Lily says... I got this in the sixties. Later when he was knighted, I updated it myself.

Gareth Hunt.

Lily says... I got this one in the queue whilst signing on. All the people behind him obviously recognized him as they were doing the hand gesture from his famous coffee advert.

Terry Christian

He was stood behind Gareth Hunt.

Dress Your Own
JEFF BANKS

Turn the tables on TV's
Jeff Banks. He's always on TV telling other
people what to wear. Now you can dress him up
and make him look ridiculous too.

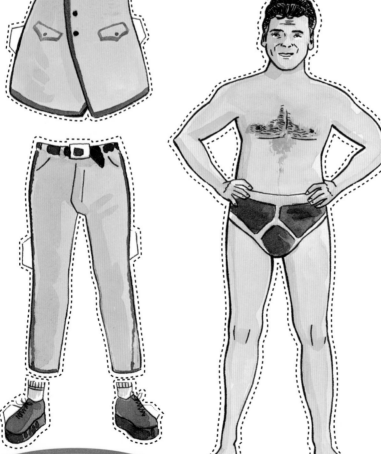

Teddy Boy

French Maid

SuperHero

Boy Scout

Cocktail Dress

Swampy

Travolta

Punk

more Popular Rumours

all rumours started by my friend Lily

The **KRAY TWINS** have always said that they would never have embarked on their criminal ways if they had known they would be portrayed on film by **SPANDAU BALLET**'s Kemp twins.

Socialite **IVANA TRUMP** is fully aware of the comical connotations of her name and laughs inwardly whenever it is mentioned.

PAULA YATES has slept with the entire cast of **EMMERDALE** including the livestock.

If you rearrange the letters in **CAPTAIN PUGWASH** you get 'A washing up pact'. If you rearrange the letters in **POSTMAN PAT** the mail goes to the wrong houses.

When **NICKY CAMPBELL** was ousted from his job on Wheel of Fortune he tried to wreak his revenge by stealing the wheel. He was stopped in the car park by a security guard called Bradley Walsh who was instantly given the job as host on Wheel of Fortune.

When made up for the first day of filming of THE ELEPHANT MAN **JOHN HURT** was misdirected to the set of BIRDS OF A FEATHER.

When anyone visits **PETE WATERMAN'S** office he makes his secretary keep them waiting while he nips out and siphons the petrol from their car.

MICKEY DOLENZ of TV's **THE MONKEES** has a life-size model of Japan that he keeps just off the coast of China.

ACORN ANTIQUES was not a real soap opera at all but a spoof version made up by comic Victoria Wood, as was **CROSSROADS**

Like many people **SIMON BATES** can't stand the sound of his own voice.

THE DIMBLEBY BROTHERS are not really brothers. Jonathan tells friends, 'With us having the same surname people just assumed we were brothers, and it stuck. Having the same parents didn't help.'

DESMOND'S was originally written as a vehicle for **DES LYNHAM.**

In London there is a retirement home for OLD RADIO 1 DJ's called Radio 2.

Irish TV presenter **GAY BYRNE** is named after an embarrassing ailment he suffered from as a boy.

Although sold here as a soap opera **NEIGHBOURS** is actually an Australian fly on the wall documentary.

WILLIAM and **HARRY** are not the royal princes' real names, they are merely pet names used within the family. Their official real names are Beavis and Butt-head.

10 THINGS YOU DIDN'T KNOW ABOUT

SHANE RIC

1 He is married to one of the Beverley Sisters.

2 He does the Daz adverts for no money whatsoever, as he really believes in the product.

3 He has turned down over thirty films including Waterworld and Schindler's List.

4 Shane insists on doing all his own stunts for Lucky Numbers.

5 The name Shane Richie means "I'll do anything on TV" in Latin.

6 Shane has three bottom cheeks, which gives him unerring confidence in crowds.

7 Shane's closest friends are all imaginary.

8 Shane loves Lion Bars.

9 Shane appeared as himself on Stars in Their Eyes but came second to Leo Sayer, who was also playing himself.

10 Shane has Tourette's Syndrome, the evidence of which is painstakingly edited out of his shows.

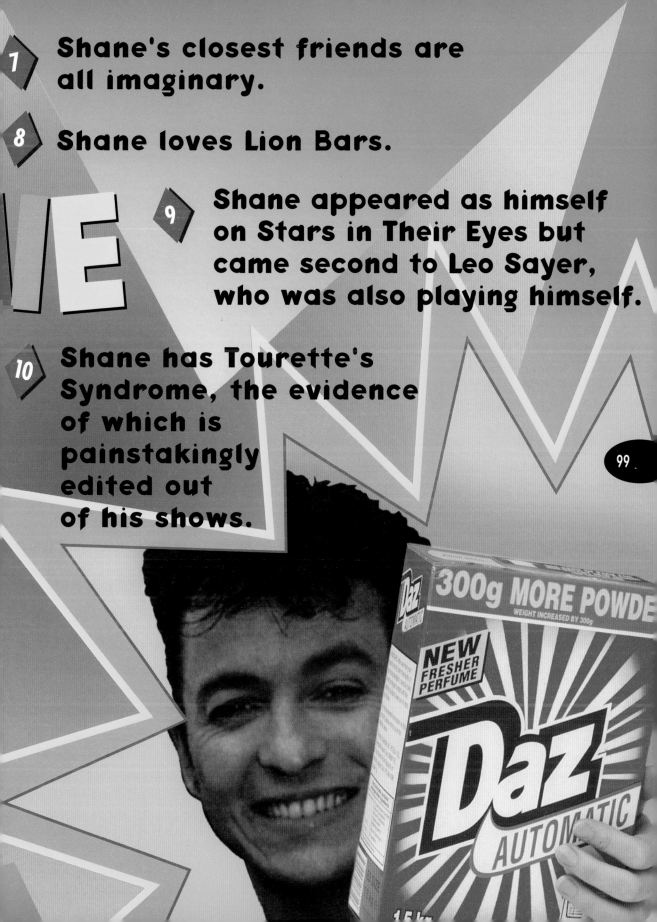

Spot the

KING'S COLLEGE OXFORD

HULL UNIVERSITY

Difference

KING'S COLLEGE OXFORD

HULL UNIVERSI

TV Celebrity

ANNUAL
Bathtime Songs

BOB
GELDOF

*The Princess
and the Frog*

**A semi-autobiographical
fantasy**

DEBBIE McGEE

102 **POSH PHOTOS
of
LADIES' BUSTERS**

PATRICK LICHFIELD

*Mmm
Betty,*

An Autobiography

STEVE COOGAN

more
NUMBERS

**Carol
Vorderman**

DANNY BAKER

Best of
**DOORSTEP
CHALLENGES**

A Collection
of Other
People's
Stories,
but my Face
on the Cover

NED SHERRIN

**WHY I SHUNNED
FAME**

**Gareth Hunt
&
Terry Christian**

BOOKCLUB

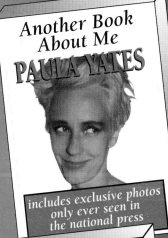

Another Book About Me
PAULA YATES

includes exclusive photos only ever seen in the national press

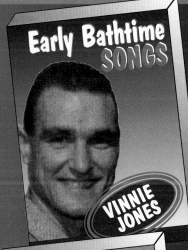

Early Bathtime
SONGS

VINNIE JONES

101 MEALS WITH MILK & MUESLI

Ulrika Jonsson

I, an actor ?

by Him who played Samir

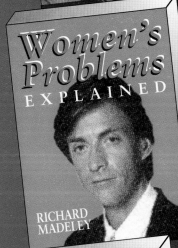

Women's Problems EXPLAINED

RICHARD MADELEY

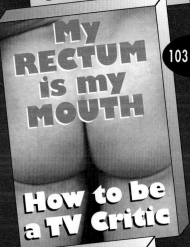

My RECTUM is my MOUTH

How to be a TV Critic

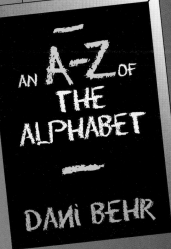

AN A-Z OF THE ALPHABET —

DANI BEHR

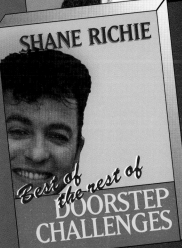

SHANE RICHIE

Best of the rest of DOORSTEP CHALLENGES

The Cat's Done a Whoopsie:

The Steve Coogan Story Continues

STEVE COOGAN

A TYPICAL DAY IN THE LIF
OF BARRY NORMAN

BARRY NORMAN

6.30 a.m. Barry wakes up and checks for a horse's head in the bed like he saw in the film The Godfather.

7.00 a.m. Showers whilst keeping one eye out for mad psychopath with a knife like he saw in the film Psycho.

7.30 a.m. Breakfast of popcorn and Kia Ora.

9.00 a.m. Drops off video at Blockbuster on way to cinema.

10.10 a.m. Takes usual chair in multiplex cinema and starts a tub of ice-cream and a large cola.

12.00 Lunch with Quentins Tarantino and Crisp. Three hot dogs with onions and mustard and another Kia Ora.

12.10 p.m. Quentin T. has a second hot dog and asks Barry if he wants the same. 'And why not?' says Barry chuckling at his own catchphrase.

2.00 p.m. Writes a review of the morning's film.

2.01 p.m. Re-enters cinema with Michael Winner. They share a box of chocolate-covered peanuts and a family bag of Revels.

4.55 p.m. Barry rings his producer, wildly excited with an idea for the name of next year's series. He wants to call it Film 98.

5.00 p.m. Another film, this time sitting next to Richard Attenborough. They share a box of Matchmakers, followed by Maltesers and wine gums.

7.00 p.m. Richard's brother David enters with a meerkat on a lead and plans to open a local ant village.

9.00 p.m. Barry calls in at Blockbuster for tonight's videos. Has the usual argument about having seen everything.

10.00 p.m. Relaxes with a bluey.

4.00 a.m. Wakes up. Pulls pants up and goes to bed.

MALCOM

My Malcolm has tried several jobs, as these photos I found of him trying on different work clothes proves only too well . . . .

The Day I Met

It was Thursday afternoon, Malcolm's half day at the library, and as a treat for him, I arranged a trip to Thorntons, the speciality confectioners in Stockport precinct. Malcolm was torn between brown or white chocolate mice, and was angling for both, and I was just gazing at the walnut clusters remembering the chocolate, nutty taste, when all of a sudden an altercation broke out at the counter between a fat elderly assistant and an elderly fat customer. I edged closer to listen properly. The fat elderly customer was complaining there were too many coffee creams in her random selection and the fat elderly assistant was saying it couldn't be the case, as they were worked out scientifically by computerized robots in Bury. At this moment myself and Malcolm Merton were

Kate Adie

pushed aside by a lady dressed in full combat gear with the uncanny air of the nation's favourite war correspondent about her. She quickly negotiated a truce involving exchanging four of the coffee creams for four plain chocolate nougats. Before we knew it, the two women were laughing heartily and showing each other their holiday pictures.

'Who was that famous lady?' Malcolm asked. 'Doesn't she play a part on BBC news?' 'Yes,' I replied, 'That was Kate Adie.' It just goes to show that even the smallest of wars can be solved by the BBC's news team. Turning to another fat assistant, I exclaimed, 'Three white chocolate mice and three brown chocolate mice. This calls for a celebration!'

TV FACTS 2

In America it is legal to marry your TV set. However, statistics prove that 4 out of 5 of these marriages end in divorce and in some states it's as many as 8 out of 10.

TV funny man Eddie Izzard has a small china figurine of a Victorian balloon seller on top of his TV set. Whenever one of his chums asks, 'What's on the telly?', the quick wit always ad libs, 'A china figurine.' This never fails to get a big laugh from Eddie and his chums.

The Queen Mother's favourite TV show is the National Lottery. Her numbers are 3, 7, 26, 31, 42 and 17. She plays both the Saturday and the mid-week games.

Richard Madeley is the only man to have said 'vaginal dryness' on national TV. He holds this record throughout Europe and North America.

If you drop a TV from the top of the Empire State Building during Coronation Street Jim Mcdonald will have said, 'So it is,' at least eighteen times before it hits the ground... so he would.

When Blind Date was thinking of having a gay special, the ITV switchboard was apparently jammed with queries.

In 1978 inmates at Strangeways Prison rioted when they were told that Barry Took would no longer be presenting Points of View. The riot was only quelled once the governors promised to see if they could instate Anne Robinson as his replacement as soon as possible.

MORE OF YOUR Views

Dear Mrs Merton

Does anybody remember Bobby Crush and are you wondering what became of the once popular pianist that shot to international stardom after winning Opportunity Knocks? Like you I was wondering the same and decided to take the initiative and track him down. This cost me several thousand pounds but eventually I found him propping up a North London bar in a pair of urine-soaked slacks.

Stephanie Davies
Marple

P.S. I can't be sure it was him, but it was definitely urine.

Dear Mrs Merton

I've counted thirty-four owls on television since the 1st January. Can anyone top this?
Yours

Phillip John Mealey
Heaton Moor

STAR LETTER

Dear Mrs Merton

I enjoyed reading page 18. Why don't you have another letters page and include mine?
Yours

Patrick Gerard
Stockport

Dear Mrs Merton

No matter how much I try, I can't get Channel 5 on my TV. If anyone else would like to know my secret, write to Andrew Harries, London.
Yours sincerely

Andy Harries
London

Dear Mrs Merton

Every time Esther Rantzen appears on the TV my dog Mitzy (Jack Russell Terrier – Spaded January 96) turns the TV over by pressing the remote. When I wrote to That's Life they didn't want to know and yet they'll have any old poodle singing along to a mouth organ. Needless to say, when your programme's on Mitzy sets the video recorder and joyfully wags her tail all the way through.

Laura Nixon
Nottingham

P.S. Is there a £10.00 prize for any letter printed?

Dear Mrs Merton

I recently saw the film Out of Africa on TV.
Yours

Kate Sullivan
Manchester

Dear Mrs Merton

Why is Fifteen to One called Fifteen to One when it's on at 4.30 p.m.? Wouldn't 12.45 p.m. be a better time? I've missed it three times this week.
Yours

Alexis Denisof
London

TFI FRIDAY

THE BIG BREAKFAST

M*A*S*H

114

BAYWATCH

TV DINNERS

I asked several TV chefs to create dishes especially for different TV programmes

CRACKER

CASUALTY

KOJAK

BIRDS OF A FEATHER

115

JIM'LL FIX IT

SOLDIER, SOLDIER

BL1ND Celebrity DATE

Over the page we've got three lovely celebrity ladies. You can only choose one of them. To help you decide we've got your three questions.

Question 1
My favourite film is The Bridge on the River Kwai because I love bridges, fords and other river crossings.
What's your favourite film and why!

Number 1 I'd have to say Free Willy or Moby Dick because I like anything in that area . . . big and gushing!

Number 2 My favourite film is West Side Story because (she stands and sings 'I want to be in America' then goes into a medley of all the other songs from West Side Story accompanied by a little dance

Number 3 I'm impressed by Polish experimental cinema. The non-sequitor expressionist imagery counterpoints ironically against

Question 2
I love romantic meals. If I were to take you out, what food would you eat?

Number 1 I like party food. Especially a bit of cheese on the end of a sausage.

Number 2 I like any kind of food. (She leaps off her chair and sings, 'Food glorious food' from Oliver)

Number 3 I like food that's been macro-biologically researched – and peas.

Question 3
Like most men, I like to have sex on the first date. How about it?

Number 1 No problem. I'm always gagging for it.

Number 2 No ... **because** (she jumps up and sings Cyndi Lauper's 'Girls Just Wanna Have Fun' with accompanying dance routine).

Number 3 No, because sex should only be part of a loving and nurturing relationship founded on mutual respect and long term bonding.

DON'T CHOOSE YET
... here's our Graham with
a quick reminder

117

Will you choose Number 1 who's a guaranteed result?
Or will it be Number 2, who frankly grates a bit?
Or will it be Number 3, who takes herself a bit seriously but,
take a tip from me, she's the best looker?

THE CHOICE IS YOURS ...

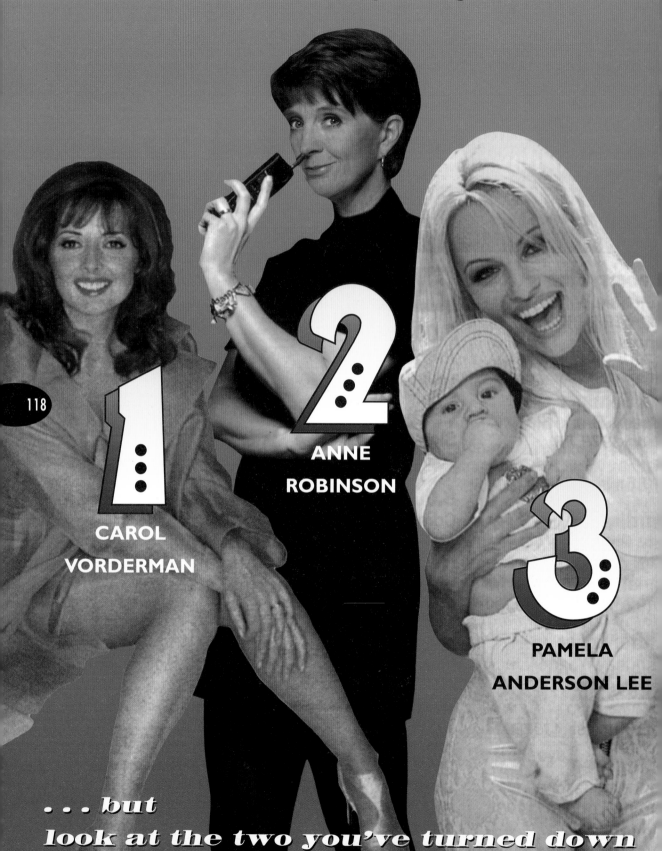

You've picked a lovely lady . . .

118

1 CAROL VORDERMAN

2 ANNE ROBINSON

3 PAMELA ANDERSON LEE

. . . but look at the two you've turned down

popular TV Jimmys

It is evident to anyone who watches TV that this media is particularly blessed with its share of **popular Jimmys**. Here's my **Top Ten**. Compare it with your own...

Jimmy Hill **(1)** **(5)** *Jimmy Cricket*

Jimmy Tarbuck **(2)** **(7)** *Jimmy Jewel*

Jimmy Savile **(3)** **(8)** *Jimmy Clitheroe*

Little Jimmy Krankie **(4)** **(9)** *Jimmy's* – the hospital drama

Jimmy Corkhill **(5)** **(10)** *Jimmy Nail*

The following didn't quite make it on account of not strictly being 'Jimmy'

*Jim Davidson, Jim McDonald,
James – the British pop music combo,
James Garner, Jamie Lee Curtis, Jamiroquai*

Jimmy Greaves
No mention

Jimmy Hill
Number one Jimmy

WHOSE TEETH ARE THEY ANYWAY?

TV is full of famous teeth but can you match these famous teeth to the TV celebrities gob they usually inhabit?

1. MICK HUCKNALL

2. MADONNA

3. CILLA BLACK

4. JIMMY HILL

5. TERRY THOMAS

6. JANET STREET-PORTER

7. KEN DODD

8. ESTHER RANTZEN

9. THE OSMONDS

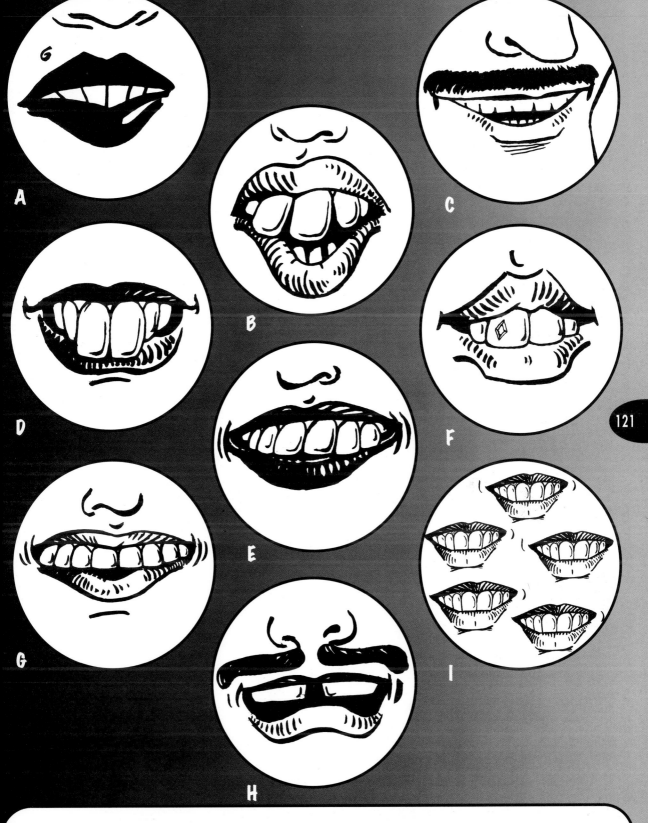

ANSWERS: 1(F), 2(A), 3(D), 4(C), 5(H), 6(E), 7(B), 8(G), 9(I)

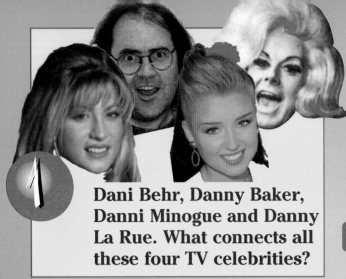

TV Quiz

1 Dani Behr, Danny Baker, Danni Minogue and Danny La Rue. What connects all these four TV celebrities?

2 Which of the following started his career as a Pontins blue coat?

a) Jeremy Paxman
b) Trevor McDonald
c) Shane Richie

3 Which of these Coronation Street stars has made their own work-out video?

a) Rosie Webster   b) Martin Platt   c) Mike Baldwin   d) Liz McDonald

4 Which Coronation Street star has not bought this exercise video?

a) Fred Elliott   b) Alf Roberts   c) Betty Williams   d) Maud

5

Who is the odd man out?

a) Jean-Claude
   Van Damme
b) Arnold
   Schwarzenegger
c) Sylvester Stallone
d) Dale Winton

6

Who has the busiest job in TV?

a) Judith Chalmers   b) Shane Richie   c) Sooty
d) The woman from Murder, She Wrote

7

Who is the most successful ginger person on TV?

a) Anne Robinson
b) Neil Kinnock
c) Rula Lenska
d) Chris Evans

8

Match the catchphrase with its celebrity mouthpiece:

a) That's magic!   i) Trevor McDonald
b) And finally...   ii) Bruce Forsyth
c) Nice to see you,   iii) Danny Baker
   to see you nice
d) I'm just a bald fat fool   iv) Paul Daniels

ANSWERS 1. Mr Merton can't stomach any of them, 2. c, 3. d, 4. d, 5. Dale Winton is the only one I've had on my show, 6. a, 7. d, 8. a=iv, b=i, c=ii, d=iii

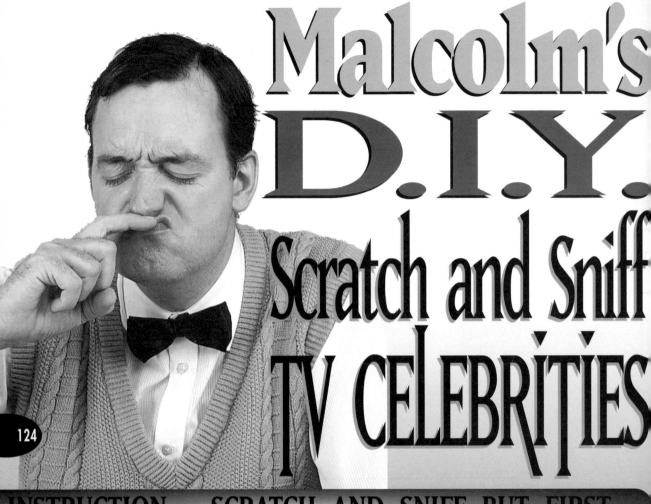

Malcolm's D.I.Y.
Scratch and Sniff TV CELEBRITIES

INSTRUCTION - SCRATCH AND SNIFF BUT FIRST...

... Place finger in bottle of Baby Bio

ALAN TITCHMARSH

ALED JONES

... Place your finger in a hymn book as if marking the page for a couple of songs

OLIVER REEI

... Sprinkle parmesan ove whole hand

... Stroke some
rhubarb

JUDY FINNIGAN

... Rest finger in a
bowl of muesli

RICHARD MADELEY

... Soak finger
in custard

ULRIKA JONSSON

PAUL DANIELS

... Rub
finger over
some Stilton

... Slide finger
through
day-old chips

DEREK JAMESON

CILLA BLACK

LOYD GROSSMAN

... Don't wash your
hands when you've
been to the toilet

... Rifle through bank-
notes, licking fingers
as you go

SOUTH BANK SHOW SPECIAL

MRS MERTON
AS SHE HAS BEEN INTERPRETTED
BY
THE GREAT ARTISTS
THROUGHOUT HISTORY

DA VINCI

VAN GOGH

PICASSO

WARHOL

MIRO

MAGRITTE

HOCKNEY

SEURAT

ATHENA

CONSTABLE

BERYL COOK

MUNCH

LOWRY

BOTTICELLI

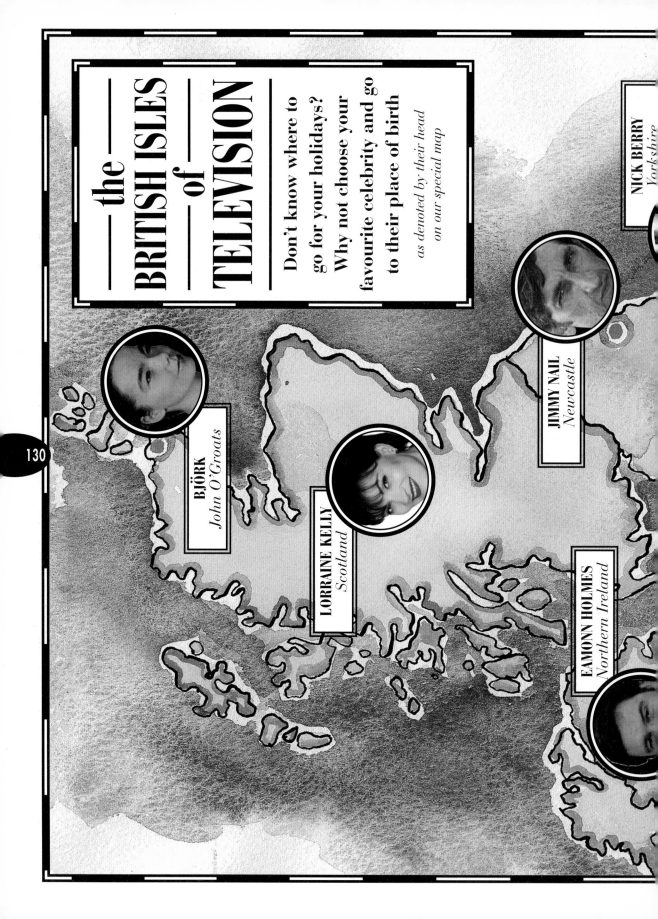

the BRITISH ISLES of TELEVISION

Don't know where to go for your holidays? Why not choose your favourite celebrity and go to their place of birth

as denoted by their head on our special map

NICK BERRY
Yorkshire

JIMMY NAIL
Newcastle

BJÖRK
John O'Groats

LORRAINE KELLY
Scotland

EAMONN HOLMES
Northern Ireland

ENGELBERT HUMPERDINCK
Leicester

BERNARD MATTHEWS
Norfolk

DAVID ESSEX
Essex

PENELOPE KEITH
South East

Manchester

ELTON JOHN
Watford

BABS WINDSOR
London

STAN BOARDMAN
Liverpool

JASPER CARROT
Birmingham

TOM JONES
Wales

BERGERAC
Jersey

DANIEL O'DONNEL
Southern Ireland

JETHRO
Cornwall

Mrs Merton's TOP all-time great programmes

DES O'CONNOR TONIGHT

Indisputably the second-best chat show on telly. Des leads the way and shows us all how to enjoy his show to the maximum. He really wrings every last drop of enjoyment out of even the smallest of jokes. Des has the uncanny ability to ask just the right questions, prompting his comedy guests into responses that are so good they should use them in their stand-up comedy routines. Des is a natural!

Operatic fun for women on the change. Pavarotti is always great value. We went to see this bearded songbird at the Royal Albert Hall. Even though we were right at the back, we could still see him as large as life. That's the beauty of him. The mark of a true professional. A friend of mine, Lily, is his number one fan but even *she* would refuse to sit next to him on a plane.

THE THREE TENORS

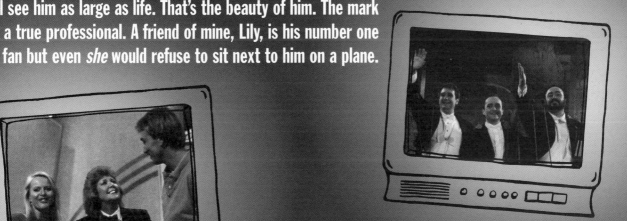

BLIND DATE

The show that's got everything tied up with a bright bow. Romance and a bit of argy-bargy at the chance to sympathize with those less fortunate in the looks department. Cilla Black puts the world of fashion to shame with her stunning outfits. Her husband Bobby Black is no doubt supporting her from the wings, just out of shot. Cilla has never forgotten her roots and neither have we. She's retained the common touch and is not afraid to display it on national television for all to see. The spontaneity of the contestants keeps this show from looking tired after it's twelve-year run.

BARRYMORE: MY KIND OF PEOPLE

He's a perennial. This series has proved there are immensely talented people amongst the general public but most especially in the Warrington area. Barrymore presents talent from unsuspecting shopping arcades throughout the nation. Who'd have thought a five-minute idea started by Esther Rantzen on That's Life could stretch to a hit series? Esther must be kicking herself! Michael Barrymore appeals to everyone and with his recent decision to become gay he appeals to even more. Keep it up Michael Barrymore!

TV COOKS

DELIA SMITH

STYLE	*Hungry man's posh crumpet*
CATCHPHRASE	*'Which makes an ideal finger buffet...'*
BEST WITH	*Cranberries*
FLAW	*Never seen with a chip pan*
MISCELLANEOUS	*She once used her husband's dentures to cut out pastry circles before she became famous on TV*

SUSAN BROOKES

STYLE : Amateur made good

CATCHPHRASE : 'So that's Chocolate Rice Krispies for you.'

BEST WITH : A toaster

FLAW : Can become violent under pressure

MISCELLANEOUS : She was origonally employed as a cleaner at Richard and Judy's mansion. She got her TV break as a reward for thinking up the title 'This Morning'

KEN HOM

STYLE : Leans toward the oriental

CATCHPHRASE : 'If that's good food, I'm a Chinaman.'

BEST WITH : A wok

FLAW : Should think of getting himself another pan

MISCELLANEOUS : When he lived in Yorkshire his friends used to call round and ask 'Is Ken Hom?'

KEITH FLOYD

STYLE	*Well-dressed tramp around town*
CATCHPHRASE	*'Where am I?'*
BEST WITH	*Cooking sherry*
FLAW	*He is unaware he is being filmed for television*
MISCELLANEOUS	*He has a recipe for stuffed peppers tattooed on his buttocks which he refuses to share with anybody*

FANNY CRADOCK

STYLE	*Old-fashioned lady who invented cooking*
CATCHPHRASE	*'I'll only do it for you if you put my Johnny on.'*
BEST WITH	*Johnny*
FLAW	*Her overuse of sexual inuendo on the words Johnny and Fanny*
MISCELLANEOUS	*Johnny came into his own after Fanny dried up on live TV*

TWO FAT LADIES

STYLE	*One fat lady and another one*
CATCHPHRASE	*(Pointing to stomach)* *'Here's one I made earlier.'*
BEST WITH	*More food than strictly speaking necessary*
FLAW	*Often egg-bound*
MISCELLANEOUS	*They're not allowed to travel in the same lift*

BETTY TURPIN

STYLE	*One fat lady*
CATCHPHRASE	*'Hotpot, lovey?'*
BEST WITH	*Potatoes, beef, peas, carrots with a pastry cover*
FLAW	*Limited menu*
MISCELLANEOUS	*Despite being on Coronation Street for 30 years she has never had a storyline*

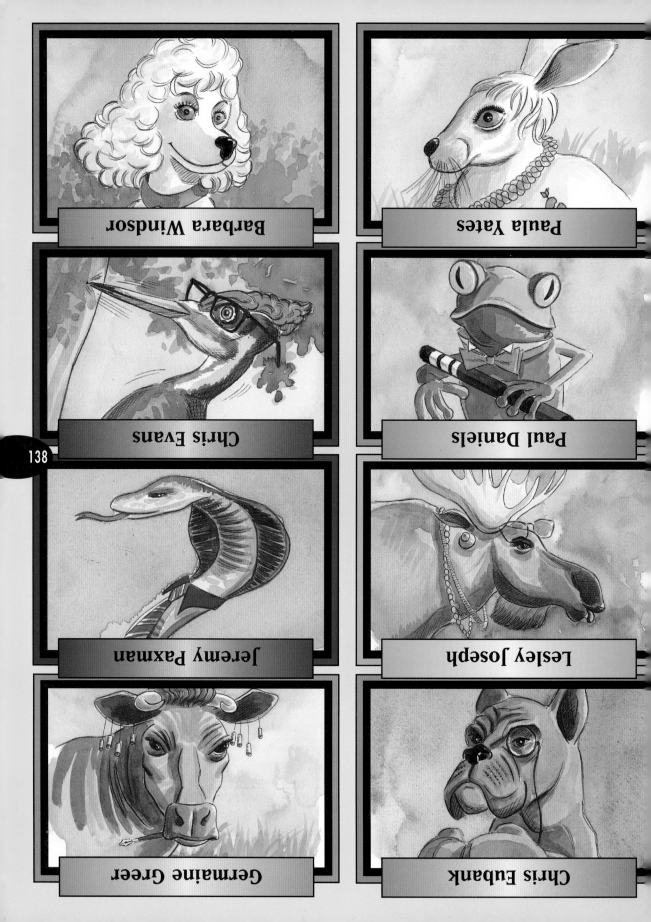

Barbara Windsor

Paula Yates

Chris Evans

Paul Daniels

Jeremy Paxman

Lesley Joseph

Germaine Greer

Chris Eubank

Peter Stringfellow

TV *Celebrity* PETS

They say you get to look like your pets but can you guess the celebrity owners of these four-legged, feathered or scaly friends?

Des Lynam

Shane Richie

JUST THE THING!

The Bill-a-Matic

Keep missing The Bill? Not any more! Simply attach the THE BILL-A-MATIC to the top of your TV set and sit back. Three times a week a realistic police siren sounds and lights flash as THE BILL-A-MATIC revolves to warn you The Bill is imminent. Available in police-blue or danger-red.

Only £9.99

Slipper Tidy

Whilst Stocks Last

Got those one-slipper blues? No dog to help you locate your other slipper? Don't despair! Get new improved SLIPPER TIDY. Ideal for those with a busy lifestyle. Clamps slippers tightly for hours on end. So don't get cold feet. Get SLIPPER TIDY. You'll feel the difference!

Only £18.99 or two for £37.98

BEFORE

AFTER

Orange-o-Tab

Pale and uninteresting? No chance of hosting a morning TV show with your wife Judy Finnigan? Try ORANGE-O-TAB. Works in minutes, lasts forever. Not available in shops.

Only £34.99

Pax-o-Mask

Too polite to unwanted visitors? Try PAX-O-MASK. As seen on TV, worn by Jeremy Paxman himself.

Only £89.99 (horribly realistic)

'It works for me...'
Jeremy Paxman

Net-o-Lifter

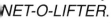

Torn between Heartbeat and your next door neighbours talking in the street? Now you can enjoy both from the comfort of your armchair with *NET-O-LIFTER*.

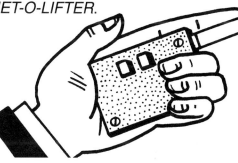

Also available SHIRT-O-LIFTER

Only £45.99

The Uphill Gardener

Back pain through bending? Been pushed too hard? Feeling stiff in the morning? You need an *UPHILL GARDENER*.

Only £15.99

Stores neatly in your back passage

Remote Control Remote Control Locator

Losing your remote control can cause concern, untold anguish and in some cases divorce as Richard Gere and Cindy Crawford can testify. It doesn't have to happen to you! Buy *REMOTE CONTROL REMOTE CONTROL LOCATOR* today. You're worth it!

Only £75.99

Available wrapped for weddings

The Portable Crumb Catcher

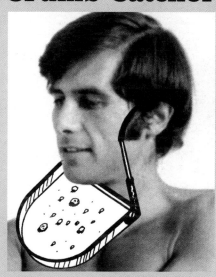

Hey, don't eat biscuits whilst watching TV? It's OK I've got *PORTABLE CRUMB CATCHER*. Comfortable and hygienic. Fits as easily as spectacles. Delivers you from the pain of crumb worries. Fully portable. Works with or without beard.

Only £14.99

(Not tested on animals)

Mrs Merton's

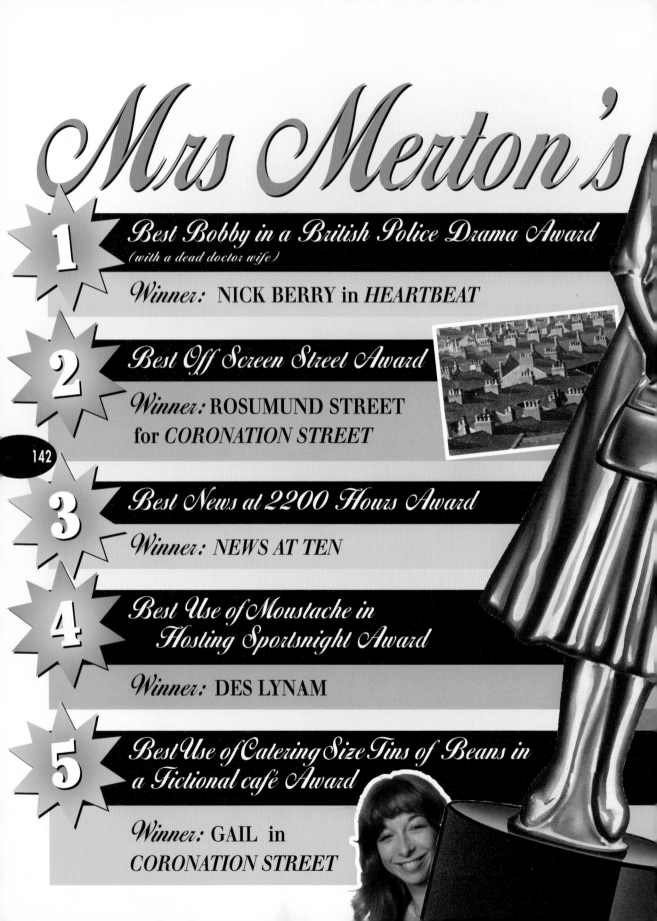

1 Best Bobby in a British Police Drama Award
(with a dead doctor wife)

Winner: NICK BERRY in *HEARTBEAT*

2 Best Off Screen Street Award

Winner: ROSUMUND STREET
for *CORONATION STREET*

3 Best News at 2200 Hours Award

Winner: NEWS AT TEN

4 Best Use of Moustache in Hosting Sportsnight Award

Winner: DES LYNAM

5 Best Use of Catering Size Tins of Beans in a Fictional café Award

Winner: GAIL in *CORONATION STREET*

142

TV Awards

The Dorothies

Most Unusual Pronunciation of the Name Deirdre Award

6

Winner: SAMIR in Coronation Street for *'DIDDERY'*

Best Presentation of Vowels and Consonants on a Channel 4 Game Show Award

7

Winner: CAROL VORDERMAN for *COUNTDOWN*

Best English Monarch in a Christmas Message Award

8

Winner: QUEEN ELIZABETH II
for *THE QUEEN'S SPEECH*

Most Persistent use of Margarita Pracatan Even When the Joke Has Worn Very Thin Award

9

Winner: CLIVE JAMES for *THE CLIVE JAMES SHOW*

Most Crowded Use of Centre Square in Celebrity Squares Award

10

Winner: LITTLE AND LARGE

With thanks to the Circus strongman Simon Prosser, the astute managerial wizardry of Jan Murphy, the wideboy charm of Rob Aslett, the fondants and fancies of Cal Lavelle, the big bag of slap of Anne Humphries, the felt tip pens of Stephen Parker, Matt 'the snapper' Squire, the immoral support of Stephanie Davies and Angela Pell, and the prayers of Momo Aherne.